CHAMBERS

KU-175-574

GUIDE TO

COMMON ERRORS

edited by
Kay Cullen

CHAMBERS

CHAMBERS
An imprint of Chambers Harrap Publishers Ltd
7 Hopetoun Crescent
Edinburgh EH7 4AY

A CIP catalogue record for this book is available from the British
Library.

We have made every effort to mark as such all words which we believe
to be trademarks.
We should also like to make it clear that the presence of a word in this
book, whether marked or unmarked, in no way affects its legal status
as a trademark.

ISBN 0550 14150 2

The British National Corpus is a collaborative initiative carried out by
Oxford University Press, Longman, Chambers Harrap, Oxford
University Computing Services, Lancaster University's Unit for
Computer Research in the English Language, and the British Library.
The project received funding from the UK department of Trade and
Industry and the Science and Engineering Research Council, and was
supported by additional research grants from the British Academy
and the British Library.

Series editor
Penny Hands

Typeset by Chambers Harrap Publishers Ltd
Printed and bound in Great Britain by
Cox & Wyman Ltd, Reading, Berkshire

Introduction

This little book is intended to help anyone who wants to know about and avoid the errors and style faults that occur most frequently in spoken and written English. In a single handy volume there is guidance on spelling, pronunciation, and grammar, as well as entries on pairs of words whose meanings or spellings may be confused – the so-called *confusables* (also spelt, incidentally, *confusibles*).

The spellings of many English words can seem to defy logic – think of *debt* /det/ and *receipt* /ri**seet**/, pronounced respectively without the *b* and the *p*. Pronunciation is therefore not, demonstrably, a reliable guide to spelling. Also, nowadays, people increasingly rely on computer spellcheckers. These are useful aids, but only in a limited way. They may help to identify typing errors, but are no real substitute for a good basic knowledge of spelling and grammar. Their limitations are all too often displayed by the ludicrous suggestions they can make when they find words they do not recognize. One of the curious aspects of using a spellchecker is that you often have to be able to spell in the first place to be certain that what the program is suggesting is correct!

Some entries in the book give guidance on **register**: for example, where a usage common in speech or informal contexts is not appropriate, say, for formal writing or business correspondence this information is given.

There are entries on style and grammar, covering the vexed question of the split infinitive, advice on whether or not a singular or plural verb should be used with words like *media* and *data*, mixed metaphors, dangling participles, and much more. In line with the modern approach, it is recognized that many of the 'rules' laid down in some older grammars and usage guides were unnecessarily prescriptive. There is no reason why, for example, a sentence should not end with a preposition. This is one of the great bugbears of purists of the old school, who apply rules borrowed from Latin grammar in a way that does not recognize that English is a living language that is changing continuously. Thus, what is perceived to be 'correct' English by one generation may be regarded as quite old-fashioned by the next. Many of the old so-called 'rules' of grammar are *flouted* (not *flaunted*) or ignored to such a degree that to continue to cling to them is rather like a small Dutch boy with the usual *complement* (not *compliment*) of fingers and toes trying to stop fifty holes in a dyke. No matter how valiant or gymnastic his efforts to hold back the flood, it will inevitably overcome him and the water will find its natural level.

The book is arranged alphabetically, making it easy to dip into and browse through. There are lots of examples showing words in context with symbols that show at a glance ✓ correct and ✗ incorrect usage. There are checklists of words whose endings are likely to cause spelling difficulty, and any differences between British and American spelling are explained in the relevant entries.

We hope that you find this book helpful and enjoyable to use. Other guides in the same series include *Guide to Punctuation*, *Guide to Effective Grammar* and *Guide to Letter Writing*.

A

a or an

The rules for which form of the indefinite article to use are:

○ *a* before words and abbreviations that begin with a consonant, eg: *a hotel* □ *a happy man* □ *a hopeless case* □ *a yacht* □ *a FIFA ruling* □ *a G8 summit* □ *a BSc.*

○ *a* before words and abbreviations that begin with a vowel, but are pronounced as though they begin with a consonant, eg: *a union* □ *a European* □ *a uniformed policeman* □ *a UN delegate.*

○ *an* before words and abbreviations that begin with a vowel, eg: *an application form* □ *an Englishman* □ *an ingenious plan* □ *an outboard motor* □ *an undertaker* □ *an e-mail* □ *an AGM.*

○ *an* before words and abbreviations that begin with a consonant, but are pronounced as though they begin with a vowel, eg: *an hour* □ *an honourable man* □ *an FDA report* □ *an HND* □ *an LP* □ *an MEP* □ *an NBC broadcast* □ *an RNLI appeal* □ *an SI unit* □ *an X-rated movie.*

abbreviate and abbreviation

Spelt with double *b*.

-able or -ible

Adjectives formed by adding the suffixes *-able* and *-ible* are frequently misspelled. Confusion may arise because the endings often sound similar when spoken. There are no simple rules that help to determine, in every instance, which of these endings is correct, so the checklist below includes many of the commonest *-able* and *-ible* words. If the word you are looking for is not included in the list or elsewhere in this book, it may help to know that the *-able* suffix is commoner; and, that most new words are formed with *-able*.

The following list shows common words ending in *-able*:

adaptable
advisable
affable
agreeable
amenable
amiable
amicable
applicable
bendable
breakable
capable
changeable
classifiable
communicable
completeable
computable
conquerable
creditable
culpable
despicable
detachable
detestable
drinkable
enviable
equitable
excusable
fashionable

flyable
forgivable
formidable
foreseeable
giveable
hireable
hospitable
implacable
indefinable
indomitable
inestimable
inevitable
inexcusable
inexorable
inferable
inflammable
insatiable
inscrutable
inseparable
intolerable
irrevocable
knowledgeable
lamentable
malleable
memorable
nameable
navigable

noticeable
palpable
payable
peaceable
persuadable
pliable
portable
predictable
preferable
probable
pronounceable
referable
reliable
repeatable
respectable
saleable
sociable
transferable
unchallengeable
unconscionable
unforgettable
unmistakable
unstoppable
usable/useable
variable
viable
vulnerable

Below is a list of common words ending in *-ible*:

accessible
adducible
admissible
audible
collapsible
combustible
compatible
comprehensible
contemptible
convertible
convincible
corruptible
defensible

deducible
depressible
destructible
digestible
dirigible
discernible
divisible
edible
eligible
exhaustible
expressible
extensible
fallible

feasible
flexible
forcible
fusible
gullible
horrible
incorrigible
indelible
indestructible
inexhaustible
inflexible
insensible
interruptible

invincible	permissible	responsible
irascible	persuasible	reversible
irrepressible	plausible	risible
irresistible	possible	sensible
legible	reducible	susceptible
negligible	reprehensible	tangible
ostensible	repressible	terrible
perceptible	reproducible	unintelligible
perfectible	resistible	visible

Note that there are some words that may be spelt with either *-able* or *-ible*. For these words the *-able* ending is more common:

collectable/collectible	correctable/correctible
detectable/detectible	extendable/extendible
includable/includible	preventable/preventible

abscess
Notice the *-sc-* in the middle, and double *s* at the end.

absorb and absorption
Remember the verb is spelt with a *b*, and the noun with a *p*.

abuse or misuse
- ○ Whether as a noun or a verb, the word *abuse* tends to be more commonly used when the intended meaning is 'use for the wrong purposes', as in: *abuse of power* □ *drug abuse* □ *He'd abused his position as a councillor in order to further his own business interests.*
- ○ Whether as a noun or a verb, *misuse* means 'use in the wrong way', as in: *the misuse of antibiotics* □ *The medical profession is accused of misusing antibiotics.*

accede
Spelt with double *c*.

➤ Compare **exceed**.

accelerate, acceleration and accelerator
Spelt with double *c* and single *l*.

accessible
Spelt with double *c*, double *s* and ending *-ible*.

accidentally
Note the ending is *-ally* (not *-ly*).

accommodate and **accommodation**
Spelt with double *c* and double *m*.

accumulate, **accumulation** and **accumulator**
Spelt with double *c* and single *m*.

accuracy and **accurate**
Spelt with double *c* and single *r*.

acknowledge
Notice the *c* before the *k*, and the ending *-edge*.

acknowledgement or **acknowledgment**
Both spellings are correct, but in BrE the form with the *e* is
more common.

acoustics
○ When the sense is 'the qualities of a space that affect how
sound is heard within it', **acoustics** is followed by a plural
verb, as in: *The acoustics here <u>are</u> better than in some modern
theatres.*
○ When the sense is 'the scientific study of sound', **acoustics**
is followed by a singular verb, as in: *Acoustics <u>is</u> a relatively
new science.*

acquaint and **acquaintance**
Remember the *c* before the *qu*, and that **acquaintance** has
the ending *-ance*.

acquiesce, **acquiescence** and **acquiescent**
Remember the *c* before the *qu*, and *-sc-* in the middle.

acquire
Remember the *c* before the *qu*.

acquit and **acquittal**
Remember the *c* before the *qu*. Notice the double *t* in
acquittal, also found in the verb forms **acquitting** and
acquitted.

across
Spelt with single *c* and double *s*.

-acy or **-asy**
Nouns that end in *-acy* and *-asy* are often misspelled.
○ When in doubt, the best guess is to use the much commoner
ending *-acy*, as in: *accuracy, adequacy, bureaucracy,*

4

conspiracy, delicacy, democracy, diplomacy, fallacy, intimacy, pharmacy, privacy and *supremacy*.

○ There are only four words that end in **-asy**: *apostasy, ecstasy, fantasy* and *idiosyncrasy*.

➤ See also **-icy** or **-isy**.

addendum

The plural is **addenda**.

adherence or adhesion

Both words have the meaning 'sticking', but they differ slightly in their use.

○ *adherence* is used for figurative senses, as in: *his adherence to the strict letter of the law*.

○ *adhesion* is used for literal senses, as in: *For heavier paper and cardboard, this type of glue gives better adhesion*.

adjacent or adjoining or contiguous

All these words share the meaning 'next to', but notice the difference in meaning.

○ *adjacent* things are beside or next to each other, but they may not be in direct contact with each other.

○ *adjoining* or *contiguous* things touch each other, usually by having an edge or boundary in common.

admission or admittance

Both words mean 'the act of entering' or 'permission to enter', but notice:

○ *admission* is used of a public place, such as a theatre: *The price of admission to the gallery is £5*.

○ *admittance* is used of a place not generally open to the public, such as a private house: *The sign on the door said, 'Private. No admittance'*.

adopted or adoptive

○ *adopted* is generally used when referring to a child, as in: *her adopted son, Rory*.

○ *adoptive* is used when referring to people who adopt a child: *adoptive parents*. It is also correct, though rare, to use *adoptive* to refer to the child.

advantage and advantageous

Note that the *e* of ***advantage*** is not dropped when adding the ending for the adjective.

adverse or averse

These words are often confused.

○ ***adverse*** means 'unfavourable, harmful, hostile', and is mostly applied to things rather than to people: *adverse weather conditions* ▢ *an adverse reaction*.

○ ***averse*** means 'disinclined' or 'opposed to'. It is often used in the negative form followed by the preposition **to**: *He's not averse to making a little extra cash on the side*.

advertise and advertisement

In BrE both words are always spelt *-ise*. However, in AmE ***advertise*** may have either the *-ise* or *-ize* ending. Note also that ***advertisement*** is usually pronounced /ad-**ver**-tis-ment/ in BrE, with the main stress on the second syllable; and, /ad-ver-**taiz**-ment/ in AmE, with the main stress on the third syllable.

advice or advise

Take care not to confuse the noun and the verb when writing these words. The verb should not be spelt with ending *-ize*.

○ ***advice*** is the noun, as in: *My advice to you is put the money in the bank immediately*.

○ ***advise*** is the verb, as in: *I advise you to put the money in the bank immediately*.

-ae- or -e-

Certain words with *-ae-* are now written without the *a*, especially in AmE. Note that BrE uses only the *-ae-* spellings for words such as *aesthetic, anaesthetic, caecum* and *haemoglobin* — the preferred AmE spellings are *esthetic, anesthetic, cecum* and *hemoglobin*. However, in BrE it is now common practice to use the spelling *medieval* instead of *mediaeval*, and *encyclopedia* instead of *encyclopaedia*.

aerial

Always with *ae-* in both BrE and AmE.

aerobics

Note that ***aerobics*** is followed by a singular verb, as in: *Aerobics <u>is</u> now a very popular form of exercise*.

aeroplane or airplane
Remember: ***aeroplane*** in BrE, and ***airplane*** in AmE.

aerosol
Always with *ae-* in both BrE and AmE.

affect or effect
Take care not to confuse these words.

○ ***affect*** is always a verb and has two main senses. The first sense means 'to influence, make a difference to', as in: *The changes won't affect the staff in this branch.* □ *I'm glad to say that none of us will be directly affected.* The second sense is rather formal and means 'to pretend', as in: *Though she affected indifference, I knew she was really very upset.*

○ ***effect*** can be a noun or a verb. As a noun it means 'result, consequence' as in: *What effect will these changes have on this branch?* □ *I was still suffering from the effects of the journey.* The verb ***effect*** is more formal and means 'to cause, to bring about', as in: *His aim was to effect a radical change in the party structure.*

affiliate and affiliation
Spelt with double *f* and single *l*.

affinity
When its meaning is 'liking, attraction or close feeling', ***affinity*** is often followed by **for** in informal and spoken English, as in: *He found he had an affinity for these people*. This is considered by many people to be incorrect. It should therefore be avoided. In formal and written English, in particular, ***affinity*** should be followed by **with**, as in: *He found he had an affinity with these people.*

afflict or inflict
Note the difference in meaning and construction.

○ ***afflict*** means 'to cause distress or discomfort', as in: *Stress afflicts people from every stratum of society* □ *He was afflicted with/by severe acne*. Note that ***afflict*** can be followed by **with** or **by**.

○ ***inflict*** means 'to impose something unpleasant or unwanted on someone', as in: *She has a tendency to inflict her troubles on others* □ *They mounted a surprise attack, and* *inflicted heavy casualties on the enemy*. Note that **inflict** is always followed by **on**.

aged

Note the different pronunciations for the different senses.

○ /**ay**-jid/ when the sense is 'elderly', as in: *aged parents*.

○ /ayjd/ when the sense is 'of a specific age', as in: *Malcolm, aged ten*.

ageing or aging

Both spellings are correct, but note that **ageing** is commoner, as well as being easier to read.

aggravate

The original meaning of **aggravate** is 'to make worse', as in: *The farmers' problems were aggravated by a prolonged drought*. **Aggravate** is also used, especially in informal English, to mean 'to irritate or annoy', as in: *It's so aggravating when people don't return your calls*. This use is considered by some to be incorrect, but it is very well established in the language and so need not be avoided except in the most formal of contexts.

aggression and aggressor

Spelt with double *g* and double *s*.

aghast

Remember the *h*, which is not sounded when spoken.

agnostic. See atheist.

airplane. See aeroplane.

alias or alibi

○ An **alias** is a false name, as in: *The fraudster has been using at least one alias*.

○ An **alibi** is proof that a person suspected of a crime was not at the scene when the crime was committed, as in: *All the possible suspects have got unshakeable alibis*.

alight

Note that the past participle and past tense of the verb is **alighted**.

align and alignment

Spelt -*lign*, though pronounced in the same way as **line**.

allege, allegation and allegedly

Spelt with double *l*. Notice also that the second *e* is dropped in **allegation**, and that **allegedly** is pronounced with four syllables /a-**lej**-id-li/.

all ready or already

In writing, take care to use the correct form.

○ **all ready** means 'completely prepared', as in: *They were all ready by 6 o'clock.*

○ **already** refers to a past action, or has the meaning 'so soon or so early', as in: *He had already had his lunch.* □ *Is it lunchtime already?*

all right or alright

Although increasingly common, **alright** is widely thought of as being incorrect. Avoid it in formal writing.

all together or altogether

In writing, take care to use the correct form.

○ **all together** means 'in a group'. Note that the two words may be separated in sentence construction, as in: *We put the sheep all together in one field.* □ *We put all the sheep together in one field.*

○ **altogether** means 'in total', as in: *How many sheep are there altogether?*

allude or elude

These words are sometimes confused or misused.

○ To **allude** to something is to speak of it indirectly, as in: *When she talked of how happy she was, we took it she was alluding to her new partner.* Notice that **allude** should not be used for something that is mentioned directly, eg:
✗ *She alluded to her holiday in France at every opportunity.*

○ To **elude** means 'to avoid or escape', as in: *Known as 'Lucky' amongst the criminal fraternity, he had eluded the police for many years.* □ *A cure for cancer continued to elude the scientists.*

Notice the double *l* in **allude**, and single *l* in **elude**.

allusion or delusion or illusion

Notice the different meanings of these words.

○ An **allusion** is an indirect reference to something, as in: *I understood this to be an allusion to his past life.*

○ A *delusion* is a false belief that is created in your own mind: *He suffers from the delusion that he's attractive to women.*

○ An *illusion* is something that creates a misleading appearance or a false belief: *The high ceiling and white walls create the illusion of space in what is, in reality, quite a small room.* Notice the double *l* in *allusion* and *illusion*, and the single *l* in *delusion*.

almond

Remember the *l*, which is not sounded when spoken.

almost

Spelt with single *l*.

alone

Notice that *alone* has a different meaning depending on where it is placed in a sentence. It can mean 'by oneself, without the company or help of others', as in: *He has lived alone since his mother died □ She always works alone.* It can also mean 'only the person or thing mentioned', as in: *He alone knows the answer to the riddle.*

already. See all ready.

alright. See all right.

also or as well or too

In formal English it is preferable to use *also* rather than *as well* or *too*, eg:

✓ *Jane was also there.*   ✗ *Jane was there as well* (or *too*).

Avoid ending a sentence with *also*, eg:

✗ *There was champagne and caviar, and smoked salmon also.*

It is not acceptable in formal English to use *also* as a synonym for **and**, eg:

✗ *There was champagne and caviar, also smoked salmon.*

alternate or alternative

Notice the different meanings and pronunciations of these words.

○ *alternate* as a verb is pronounced /**awl**-ter-nayt/ and means 'to switch between two things repeatedly', as in: *Her mood alternates between elation and deep despair.* As an adjective, *alternate* is pronounced /awl-**ter**-nit/ and refers to things that come after each other by turns, or which happen on every second occasion, as in: *alternate periods of flooding and drought* □ *She visits her parents on alternate Saturdays during term time.* Notice that in AmE the adjective **alternate** is used where BrE would use the adjective **alternative**, eg: (AmE) *an alternate route* □ (BrE) *an alternative route.*

○ **alternative** is pronounced /awl-**ter**-na-tiv/. As a noun, it means 'one of several possibilities or choices', as in: *There are several equally attractive alternatives.* As an adjective, **alternative** refers to something that offers a choice between two possibilities, as in: *an alternative method of payment.*

although and though

There is little difference between these words. Note, however, that while one may be substituted for the other in many instances, only **though** can be used at the end of a sentence, as in the following example: *We finished in good time. It was very hard work, though.*

altogether. See all together.

amend or emend

These words are often confused.

○ **amend** means 'to alter or add to something in order to improve or correct it', as in: *The committee recommended to the government that the law be amended.*

○ **emend** means 'to correct errors in', and applies specifically to written material, as in: *He emended the typescript before sending it to the printers.*

amiable or amicable

Both words convey the idea of friendliness, but **amiable** is used to refer to people and **amicable** to actions or situations.

○ **amiable** means 'friendly, pleasant or good-natured', as in: *Many people are afraid of him, though I found him to be perfectly amiable.*

○ **amicable** means 'done in a friendly way', as in: *The discussions were amicable, though business-like.*

among(st). See between.

amoral or immoral

Notice the difference in meaning.

○ **amoral** is used to refer to people who do not believe that any moral code exists, and therefore there is no such thing as right and wrong.

○ *immoral* refers to a person or action considered to be wrong or evil by people generally.

an. See **a**.

anaesthetic
Always spelt with *-ae-* in BrE.

analogous. See **similar**.

analyse, analysis and analyst
Take care to spell all these words with *y* (not *i*), and remember never to use the AmE spelling **analyze** in BrE. Note that the plural of *analysis* is **analyses**.

and
The informal usage in which *and* is placed after words such as **try** and **sure** is not acceptable in formal contexts. Use **to** instead.

✗ *Try and eat a little more.*   ✓ *Try to eat a little more*
✗ *Be sure and leave early.*   ✓ *Be sure to leave early.*

annex and annexe
Note that *annex* is the verb and *annexe* is the noun.

annihilate and annihilation
Remember the double *n*, the *h* in the middle, and the single *l*.

anonymous
Spelt with *y* (not *i*).

answer
Remember the *w* in the middle, which is not sounded when spoken.

ante- or anti-
In writing, do not confuse these prefixes, which have different meanings.

○ *ante-* means 'before', as in: *antecedent, antediluvian, antenatal*.

○ *anti-* is more common and means 'against or opposed to' and 'opposite to', as in: *antibiotic, anticlimax, anticlockwise, antifreeze, antisocial, anti-war*.

antenna

There are two plurals, **antennae** and **antennas**, but note they are used for different senses.

○ *antennae* is used for insects' sensing organs or feelers.

○ *antennas* is used for aerials.

anti-. See **ante-**.

anticipate

Notice the *c*.

antisocial. See **unsociable**.

anyone or any one

In writing, take care to use the correct form.

○ *anyone* is used in the same way as **anybody** to refer to an unspecified person, as in: *Is there anyone there?*

○ *any one* always refers to a particular group of people or things mentioned, as in: *There were three candidates who impressed me: I would offer any one of them the job.*

any time

This is always written as two words.

anyway or any way

In writing, take care to use the correct form.

○ *anyway* is an adverb and can mean 'in any case' or 'in spite of that', as in: *I didn't get the job; anyway, the hours wouldn't have suited me.* □ *He isn't one of my favourite directors, but I went to see the film anyway.*

○ *any way* means 'by any means or manner', as in: *You look worried; can I help in any way?* □ *Do it any way you like.*

apologize and apologise

Notice the single *p*, and the second *o* in the middle. Both endings are correct, though the *-ise* ending is not used in AmE.

appal or appall

In BrE the infinitive **appal** and the 3rd person present singular **appals** have only one *l*. In AmE these have double *l*, as do the present participle **appalling** and past participle/past tense **appalled** in BrE.

apparatus

Notice the double *p*, the single *r* and the single *t*. There are two plurals: **apparatus** and (less commonly) **apparatuses**.

apparent and apparently

Spelt with double *p* and ending *-ent(ly)*.

appendix

There are two plurals: **appendixes** and **appendices**.

○ *appendixes* is used in the anatomical sense.

○ *appendices* is used for extra sections at the ends of some books. *Appendixes* is also sometimes used for this sense.

appreciate and appreciation

Notice the double *p*, the *e* and the *c*.

appropriate

Remember the double *p* at the beginning.

apt. See prone.

aquarium

There are two plurals: **aquariums** and (less commonly) **aquaria**.

-ar. See -er.

arbiter or arbitrator

○ An *arbiter* is a person whose opinions are respected and followed, as in: *an arbiter of taste and fashion*.

○ An *arbitrator* is a person who is chosen to decide between two people or groups in a dispute, as in: *He acts as arbitrator in industrial disputes*. Note that it is also correct to use *arbiter* in this sense.

argue and argument

Notice that the *e* of *argue* is dropped in *argument*.

as. See like.

ascent or assent

Notice the different spellings of these words.

○ *ascent* is a noun and means 'a climb or act of rising to a higher level', as in: *the first ascent of Everest □ his rapid ascent to the top job in the company*

○ *assent* is a noun and a verb meaning 'agreement' and 'to agree': *Luke had taken her silence for assent. □ Reluctantly, she assented.*

ascertain

Pronounced /a-ser-**tayn**/ with the stress on the third syllable.

asphyxiate and asphyxiation

Remember is the *-ph-y-x-* in the middle.

assassin, assassinate and assassination

Remember the first and the second double *s*. A memory aid is to think of two donkeys, one following the other.

assistance and assistant

Spelt with double *s* at the beginning, and single *s* in the middle.

asthma

Note the *th* in the middle, which is not sounded when spoken.

assume. See presume.

as well. See also.

-asy. See -acy.

atheist or agnostic

○ An *atheist* is someone who does not believe that God exists.

○ An *agnostic* is a person who believes it is impossible to prove if God exists.

athletics

Notice that **athletics** is followed by a singular verb, as in: *Athletics is his passion, though he also enjoys football*.

attach. See detach.

aural or oral

Notice the different meanings.

○ *aural* means 'relating to the ear', or 'listening', as in: *an aural test*.

○ *oral* means 'relating to the mouth' or 'spoken', as in: *oral hygiene □ The students have done the written paper already: the oral part of the exam is on Wednesday*.

authoritarian or authoritative

Notice the different meanings.

○ *authoritarian* means 'demanding obedience', as in: *an authoritarian regime*.

○ *authoritative* means 'having authority', as in: *an authoritative source*.

averse. See **adverse**.

avert or **avoid** or **evade**

These words are sometimes confused.

○ **avert** is a rather formal word and means 'to prevent something unpleasant happening' or 'to move away from something unpleasant', as in: *The threatened crisis was thus averted.* □ *She averted her eyes*.

○ **avoid** means 'to keep away from' or 'to take the necessary action to prevent something unpleasant happening', as in: *The lorry swerved to avoid the sheep.* □ *He avoided her gaze.* □ *to avoid a damaging strike*.

○ **evade** has a similar meaning to **avoid** in the sense of taking action to escape from or dodge something awkward or unpleasant, but it usually implies that the action taken is underhand or involves a trick of some sort, as in: *It is illegal to evade tax.* □ *You're trying to evade the question, minister*.

awesome, awful and **awfully**

Notice that there is an *e* in **awesome**, and that **awfully** has double *l*.

B

bachelor

Remember: there is no *t* before the *ch*, despite the pronunciation.

bacillus

The plural is **bacilli**.

backward or backwards

Backward can be an adverb or an adjective. *Backwards* is only an adverb. In BrE the more usual adverb is *backwards*, while in AmE it is *backward*, as in: (BrE) *He toppled backwards and his head hit the wall.* □ (AmE) *He toppled backward and his head hit the wall.*

bacteria

Remember that *bacteria* is the plural of **bacterium** and should not be used with a singular verb:
- ✗ *The type of bacteria has not yet been identified.*
- ✓ *The type of bacterium has not yet been identified.*
- ✓ *The bacteria have not yet been identified.*

bade. See bid.

baggage

Remember the double *g*, followed by *-age*.

bail or bale

Note the spellings for the different senses.

- ○ *bail* is money paid to a court. *Bails* are the short pieces of wood across the top of a cricket stump.
- ○ A *bale* is a bundle of hay. As a verb, *bale* and *bale out* mean 'to scoop water out of a boat', and *bale out* can also mean 'to jump from an aircraft in an emergency'.

baited or bated

Notice the different spellings for the different meanings.

- A ***baited*** trap is one that has bait on or in it.
- ***bated*** means 'held back', as in: *We stood waiting with bated breath*.

balk or baulk

Both spellings are correct, but ***baulk*** is more common.

barely, hardly and scarcely

In sentence construction, it is incorrect to follow these words with **than**. Use **when** or **before** instead, as in: *They had barely got the tent up when a blizzard began.* ▫ *The film had hardly started before the fire alarm rang.* ▫ *We had scarcely begun our discussion when Keith was called away.*

➤ See also **double negatives**.

basically

Remember the ending is spelt *-ally* (not *-ly*).

In formal and written English, avoid using ***basically*** for emphasis or to introduce a statement, eg: *Well, basically, I don't think it's a very good idea.*

basis

The plural is **bases**.

bated. See baited.

bath or bathe

Notice that in BrE ***bath*** is used as a verb as well as a noun and means 'to wash the whole body in a bath' or 'to wash someone in a bath'. AmE uses the verb ***bathe*** for these senses. In BrE ***bathe*** means 'to swim' or 'to wash a part of the body'.

battalion

Spelt with double *t* and single *l*.

baulk. See balk.

beautiful

Remember the correct order of the vowels *-e-a-u-*.

because

In certain constructions the use of ***because*** may be considered non-standard English, or can result in ambiguity. For written English, in particular, note the following:

- ***because*** should not be used to introduce a subordinate clause referring back to **reason** or **reason why** in the main clause:

✗ *The reason (why) she didn't get an interview was because she was too young.*

✓ *The reason (why) she didn't get an interview was that she was too young.*

○ ***because*** should be avoided in negative constructions where the meaning may be ambiguous, eg: *She didn't object to being photographed because she is shy.* This can mean 'She is too shy to object' or 'She objected, not because she is shy, but for some other reason'.

because of or due to or owing to

○ ***because of*** and ***owing to*** are used in phrases that refer to the verb (underlined in the following examples): *The meeting was <u>cancelled</u> because of the rail strike.* □ *Owing to the bad weather, most of the fishing fleet <u>returned</u> to port.*

○ The rules of traditional grammar dictated that ***due to*** could only be used to refer to a noun, as in: *Their <u>success</u> was due to prudent financial management.* However, it is now widely accepted that ***due to*** can also refer to a verb, as in: *The window frame has to be <u>replaced</u> due to damage to the double glazing unit.*

beggar

Remember the ending is spelt *-ar* (not *-er*).

begin, beginner and beginning

Notice the double *n* in ***beginner*** and ***beginning***. The past tense of ***begin*** is **began** and the past participle is **begun**.

begin or commence or start

Note the differences in usage.

○ In written English ***begin*** is more formal than ***start***, and ***commence*** is more formal than ***begin***, as in: *You may start.* □ *You may begin.* □ *You may commence.*

○ ***begin*** or ***start*** may be followed by the infinitive or the *-ing* form of a verb. Notice, however, that the *-ing* form is more common when referring to an activity that goes on for a long period of time, as in: *She began to make friends as soon as she arrived.* □ *The bush started to show signs of life.* □ *He began playing the violin when he was six.* □ *The men started painting the bridge in April.* ***Commence*** is always followed by the *-ing* form, as in: *The lawyer for the defence will now commence cross-examining the witness.*

behaviour or behavior

Spelt with the *u* in BrE and without the *u* in AmE.

beige

Remember the *e* comes before the *i*. Pronounced /bayj/.

believe

Note that the *i* comes before the *e*.

beloved

As a noun, pronounced with three syllables with the stress on the second syllable /bi-**luv**-id/.

beside or besides

○ ***beside*** is a preposition and means 'next to, at the side of', as in: *Duncan is the tall man standing beside my father.*

○ ***besides*** means 'in addition to', as in: *Do you know any good plumbers besides old Mr Clark?* ***Beside*** is sometimes used for this sense, but this usage should be avoided in formal English.

between or among(st)

There are several common errors in the use of ***between***:

○ ***between*** should always be followed by object pronouns (i.e. **me**, **you**, **him**, **her**, **them**), as in: *There's some sort of feud going on between them.* When there are two pronouns, take care not to change the second to a subject pronoun, eg:
✗ *Between you and I, I think he's gone a little mad.*
✓ *Between you and me, I think he's gone a little mad.*

○ ***between*** should never be followed by **each** or **every** and a singular noun or noun phrase, eg:
✗ *They rested for an hour between each performance.*
✓ *They rested for an hour between performances.*
✗ *The congregation sat down again between every hymn.*
✓ *The congregation sat down again between hymns.*

○ ***between*** should be followed by **and**, never by **or**, as in:
✓ *Must I choose between having a family and a career?*
✗ *Must I choose between having a family or a career?*
✓ *The guests are due to arrive between five and six.*
✗ *The guests are due to arrive between five or six.*

○ ***between*** should not be repeated before the second element of a pair where the first element is long and is followed by **and**, eg:

✗ *There's a world of difference between exploring the wilderness with an experienced guide who knows the terrain well enough to keep you out of danger and between wandering off by yourself.*

Notice the following points relating to the use of **between** and **among(st)**:

○ **between** is used to describe the relationship of only two people or things, which are often named or given a number, as in: *The estate was divided between Hugh and George.* □ *I want to share the money equally between my two sons.* □ *The sugar is on the top shelf, between the rice and the coffee.*

○ **among** or **amongst** is usually used when there are more than two people or objects, especially when these are not named individually, as in: *They came upon a little house amongst the trees.* □ *Share the sweets among your classmates.* □ *The jar is on the top shelf, amongst the other food containers.* However, it is also now common and quite acceptable to use **between** for more than two, as in: *I want to share the money between John, Peter and Louise.*

bid, biddable and bidding

When the sense is 'to stay, tell or command' the past tense of **bid** is **bade**, pronounced /bad/ or /bayd/. Notice the double *d* in the adjective **biddable** and the present participle **bidding**.

billiards

Note that **billiards** is followed by a singular verb, as in: *Billiards is less popular than snooker.*

binoculars

Note that **binoculars** takes a plural verb, as in: *My binoculars are in the glove compartment.*

biscuit

Memorize the letter combination *-c-u-i-t*.

blamable or blameable

Both spellings are correct, but notice that the form with the *e* is easier to read.

blasphemous and blasphemy

Notice the *ph*, pronounced /f/.

blond or blonde

Both words can be adjectives or nouns. These words are borrowed from French and so, unlike English adjectives, have masculine and feminine forms: **blond** is masculine and **blonde** is feminine, as in: *He was blond as a child.* □ *She's a gorgeous blonde.* However, the use of the masculine form in '*She has blond hair*' is considered acceptable in English because the adjective describes the noun 'hair'.

bolder or boulder

Take care not to confuse the spellings of these words.

○ **bolder** is an adjective meaning 'more bold'.

○ A **boulder** is a large rock.

both

Note that **both** should be followed by **and**, not **as well as**, eg:

✓ *She is both depressed and angry.*

✗ *She is both depressed as well as angry.*

It is not correct to use **both** with more than two objects, eg:

✗ *She is both depressed, angry and afraid for the future.*

boundary

Note the *u* and the *-ary* ending.

breath or breathe

Note the *-ea-* in the middle. Remember that **breath** is the noun and **breathe** is the verb, as in: *She put her head out of the water and took a deep breath.* □ *He was finding it difficult to breathe.* The present participle of the verb is **breathing** and the past tense/past participle is **breathed**.

brilliance and brilliant

Note the double *l* and the *-ance* and *-ant* endings.

broach or brooch

Notice the different meanings.

○ **broach** can be a verb or a noun. The commonest meaning of the verb is 'to raise (a subject)', as in: *I was reluctant to broach the subject of expenses.*

○ A **brooch** is a piece of jewellery.

brochure

Spelt with *ch* (not *s*).

bruise

Remember the *i* following the *u*.

bulk or most or majority

It is correct to use the phrase 'the **bulk** of' before an uncountable noun, as in: *The bulk of our overseas trade is with the Far East*. However, when the noun is countable, use '**most** of' or 'the **majority** of', eg: *Most of the girls speak French.* ❑ *The majority of cars on the road are carrying only one or two people.*

buoy, buoyancy and buoyant

Notice the *-uo-* in these words, and the *-ancy* and *-ant* endings.

burglar and burglary

Notice the *-ar* and *-ary* endings.

bus

The plural in BrE is **buses**. In AmE, the plural is also spelt **busses**.

business

Note the *u* and the double *s*. Also remember the *i*, which is not sounded when spoken.

C

caffeine
Notice the double *f*, and that the *e* comes before the *i*.

calendar
Remember *e* (not *a*) in the second syllable, and *a* (not *e*) in the third.

campaign
Remember the letter sequence *-p-a-i-g-n*.

can or may
Some traditionalists continue to adhere to the rule that **may** should be used to convey the sense of permission being sought or granted; and, that **can** should only be used when the sense has the connotation of ability or possibility, as in the following examples:
> ✓ *May I leave the table now?*
> ✓ *Yes, you may borrow my umbrella.*
> ✗ *Can I have a new computer?*
> ✓ *He can* [= is able to] *contact us by radio.*

However, **can** is now used for all senses, including those with the sense of allowing or permission. In fact, in some contexts the sense of permission is made clearer by using **can** instead of **may**. In the example, '*Ladies may use the saunas on Tuesday and Thursday afternoons*' notice the ambiguity created by the use of **may**. It is unclear if the intended meaning is that ladies are allowed to use the saunas on these days (but not at other times), or whether there is a chance that they will be using the saunas.

➤ See also **could**.

cancel and cancellation
In BrE, the *l* of **cancel** is doubled for the noun, and for the verb forms **cancelling** and **cancelled**. In AmE, the spellings

canceled and **canceling** are also used for the verb forms.

can not or cannot

In BrE, *cannot* must be used, except in the few instances where **not** is linked to the following word in a way that requires that it be separated from **can**, as in: *The drug can not only alleviate the physical symptoms of the disease but also gives patients a feeling of wellbeing.*

In AmE *can not* is the preferred form, where BrE would use *cannot*.

In all but the most formal contexts, *cannot* may be shortened to **can't**.

canoe and canoeing

The *e* of *canoe* is not dropped for the present participle *canoeing*.

canvas or canvass

Note the difference between these words.

○ *canvas* is a strong fabric.

○ *canvass* is a verb meaning 'to ask for votes or support', as in: *They were canvassing for the Liberal Democrats*.

capsize

Always spelt with a *z* (never with an *s*).

carburetter or carburettor

In BrE, both spellings are correct. Note the single *r*, and the double *t* (but for AmE a single *t*).

career

There is only one *r* in the middle of this word.

caress

There is only one *r* in the middle of this word. Notice also the double *s*.

carriage

Notice the double *r* and the *i*.

cashier

Take care to spell this word with *-ier* (not *-eer*).

casual, casually and casualty

Remember the *u* before the second *a*, which is sometimes not sounded when spoken.

catarrh

Notice the *-rrh* spelling (from the ancient Greek word *rheein* = to flow).

-ce or -se

Words with these endings are often misspelled. There are some broad guidelines that can help when there is doubt about which ending should be used.

○ Nouns related to adjectives with **-ant** or **-ent** endings are spelt with the *-ce* ending, eg: *different/difference, correspondent/correspondence, ignorant/ignorance, assistant/ assistance*.

○ Words whose endings are pronounced with a /z/ sound are written with *-se*, eg: *advise, devise, exercise, expertise, franchise, house* (verb), *refuse* (verb), *revise*.

➤ See also **-ize** or **-ise**.

○ Words whose endings are pronounced with an /s/ sound following a vowel are usually spelt with *-ce*, eg: *advice, choice, deduce, device, justice, mice, office, price, race, rejoice, voice*. However, note the following exceptions: *chase, house* (noun), *mouse, obtuse, profuse, promise, refuse* (noun).

○ Words pronounced with an /s/ sound following a consonant can present the greatest problems because their spellings may be *-ce* or *-se*. The following checklist includes some of the commonest words in this category.

advance	dense
commerce	endorse
finance	immense
offence	intense
pronounce	recompense
preference	response
romance	tense

➤ For differences in BrE and AmE spelling see individual alphabetical entries.

-cede or -ceed or -sede

These endings sound alike and are sometimes confused. Note the following as an aid to correct spelling:

○ The majority of words pronounced in this way end with *-cede*, eg: *accede, concede, precede, recede, secede*.

○ There are only three words that end in *-ceed*: *exceed, proceed, succeed.*

○ Only one word ends in *-sede*: *supersede.*

ceiling

The spelling of this word follows that well-known rule, '*i* before *e*, except after *c*'.

cemetery

Take care not to leave out the third *e*, which is usually not sounded when spoken.

censer or censor or censure

Note the different meanings. The spellings of the verbs *censor* and *censure* are often confused.

○ a *censer* is a container in which incense is burnt.

○ a *censor* is a person who examines books, letters or films and decides whether they contain any harmful material that must be deleted or that makes them unsuitable for publication, etc. *Censor* is also a verb, as in: *His letter had been so heavily censored that only 'Dear Alice' and his signature could be read.*

○ *censure* is criticism or blame. It can also be a verb, as in: *A civil servant was censured for leaking the story to the press.*

ceremonial or ceremonious

Notice the different meanings.

○ *ceremonial* is an adjective and a noun and means '(for, involving or suited to) a formal ceremony', as in: *ceremonial robes □ the ceremonial of the investiture.*

○ *ceremonious* is an adjective and means 'excessively formal or polite', as in: *He swept his hat from his head with a flourish and gave a low ceremonious bow.*

-ch or -tch

In words ending with a /ch/ sound, the following guidelines can be used to determine whether the *-ch* or the *-tch* ending is correct. Note that these rules cannot be applied to placenames, or to words where the final **ch** is not pronounced /ch/, as in *epoch* and *loch*.

○ If there is a consonant before the /ch/ sound, the spelling will be *-ch*, eg: *arch, branch, church, filch, search, squelch, torch.*

- ○ If there is a vowel sound made up of more than one letter before the /ch/ sound, the spelling will be **-ch**, eg: *approach, brooch, couch, debauch, mooch, screech, teach, touch*. Note the single exception: *aitch*.
- ○ If there is a vowel sound of a single letter before the /ch/ sound, the spelling will be **-tch**, eg: *catch, dispatch, fetch, hutch, scratch, watch, witch*. Note that there are several exceptions to this rule, eg: *attach, detach, enrich, much, ostrich, rich, sandwich, spinach, such, which*.

chamois
Note that the animal should be pronounced /**sham**-wah/ and the leather /**sha**-mi/.

change and changeable
Notice that the *e* of **change** is not dropped when adding the ending for the adjective **changeable**.

character, characteristic and characteristically
Remember all these words start with *ch*. Also notice that **characteristically** ends with *-ally* (not *-ly*).

chasm
Notice this word is spelt *cha-* (not *ca-*).

chief, chiefly and chieftain
Remember the *i* comes before the *e*.

childish or childlike
Both these words mean 'of or like a child', and are applied to adults. Notice that **childish** is a term of disapproval, but **childlike** is usually used in an approving or neutral way, as in: *That was a really childish thing to do!* □ *She has a childlike quality that makes her ideal for the part.* □ *He was childlike in his naivety.*

chimney
The plural is **chimneys**.

chocolate
Remember the second *o*, which is usually not sounded when spoken.

chrysanthemum
A favourite in spelling tests. Remember the *ch*, the *y*, and the *-the-*.

-cion. See **-tion**.

classic or classical

These words are used in different ways.

○ The noun and adjective **classic** denotes a work of literature or art of high quality and lasting value, as in: *that classic of Russian literature, 'War and Peace'* □ *a classic Hitchcock movie*. As an adjective, **classic** is also used to refer to something that is typical of its kind, as in: *one of the classic signs of drug dependency* □ *a classic example of a mixed metaphor*. Other adjectival senses of **classic** include 'simple and elegant', as in: *a variation of the classic little black dress*. The plural noun **classics** denotes ancient Greek and Latin studies, as in: *Nowadays, a smaller percentage of university students study classics*.

○ **classical** is an adjective and means 'of or relating to classics or ancient Greece or Rome', as in: *a classical education* □ *classical Greek drama*. It is also used to refer to music that is serious and formal rather than light or modern; to art and architecture of, or influenced by, the ancient Greeks and Romans and characterized by restraint, order and discipline rather than innovation or emotion; and, more generally, to something that is well established or standard, as in: *a departure from classical one-nation Toryism*.

clean or cleanse

Both words mean 'to remove dirt from', but **cleanse** is often applied to a part of the body and has the added connotation that the cleaning is a very thorough process, as in: *Taking only fruit juice and water for two or three days will cleanse the system of impurities*.

cliché

A **cliché** is a set phrase or combination of words that has become degraded by overuse, eg: *He was over the moon.* □ *the fact of the matter is …* □ *at the end of the day*. A speaker who uses too many clichés risks giving the impression that their ability to express themselves is limited.

clientele

Note the ending is spelt *-ele* (not *-el* or *-ell*).

climatic or **climactic**

These adjectives should not be confused.

○ *climatic* means 'of or relating to climate', as in: *The phenomenon known as El Nino has been blamed for the unusual climatic conditions being experienced in various parts of the world.*

○ *climactic* means 'of or like a climax', as in: *The climactic scene is preceded by a crescendo of sound from the orchestra.*

clique

Pronounced /kleek/.

coercion

Notice the *-cion* ending.

coherence or **cohesion**

Both words have the general sense of 'sticking together', but note the different usage.

○ *coherence* is used of the degree to which ideas, etc fit together logically, and of the degree to which social systems or organizations function effectively as a whole, as in: *The government's policies appear to lack consistency and coherence.* □ *He argues that the coherence of traditional family life has been threatened by feminism.*

○ *cohesion* is used for the literal sense of sticking together, and for the figurative sense of unanimity or closeness within a group, as in: *the cohesion of molecules* □ *The cohesion of the Cabinet was torn apart over the issue of the minimum wage.*

collaborate and **collaborator**

Note the double *l* and the single *b*.

collapse and **collapsible**

Note the double *l* and the *-ible* ending.

colossal

Remember: single *l* followed by double *s*, and ending *-al*.

commemorate and **commemoration**

Notice the double *m* followed by single *m*.

commence. See **begin**.

commit and **commitment**

Notice that the verb forms **committing** and **committed** have a double *t*, but *commitment* has only one *t*.

committee

Spelt with double *m*, double *t* and double *e*.

common or mutual

Traditionally, these words could not be used interchangeably, and for formal English it is best to keep the distinction as follows:

○ **common** means 'belonging to or shared by two or more people', as in: *a common language* □ *common knowledge* □ *Our common interest in botany created a bond between us.*

○ **mutual** means 'given by each to the other or others involved, reciprocal', as in: *mutual respect* □ *The feeling was mutual.*

comparable or comparative

Do not confuse these words.

○ **comparable** means 'of the same kind, of the same scale, to the same degree, etc', as in: *You won't find wine of comparable quality throughout Italy.*

○ **comparative** means 'judged by comparing with something else', as in: *In the periods of comparative calm between bombardments, they tried to get some much-needed sleep.*

comparative

Notice the spelling: *a* (not *i*) in the third syllable.

compare to or compare with

Note the difference in meaning.

○ **compare to** means 'to liken to or characterize as similar to', as in: *He compared the flight to a ride on a rollercoaster.*

○ **compare with** means 'to study or examine in detail, so as to find similarities or differences', as in: *How does Tuscany compare with the South of France?* □ *Compare modern methods of agriculture with those of the last century.*

comparison

Notice the spelling: *i* (not *a*) in the third syllable.

compel or impel

Notice the difference in meaning.

○ **compel** means 'to force', and is usually used when the force is being applied by someone or something else, as in: *They were compelled to work in the fields.*

○ *impel* means 'to drive or urge', and is usually used when someone is being driven by their own needs or desires to do something, as in: *Fear of failure impelled him to greater and greater efforts.*

compendium

There are two plurals: **compendiums** and **compendia**.

complacent or complaisant or compliant

These words are sometimes confused.

○ *complacent* means 'self-satisfied or confident in your own abilities', as in: *It's dangerous to get too complacent in today's cut-throat market.*

○ *complaisant* means 'willing to do what others want, especially in a cheerful relaxed way', as in: *Her father rarely allowed her to have her own way; it was her mother who was the complaisant one.*

○ *compliant* also means 'willing to do what others want', but usually also implies 'giving in to someone', as in: *He said he was on the lookout for a rich and compliant wife.*

complement or compliment

These words have the same pronunciation but note the different meanings:

○ a *complement* is something that completes or perfects: *A dry white wine is an ideal complement to fish.* In grammar, *complement* denotes a word or phrase added after the verb to complete the predicate of a sentence.

○ a *compliment* is an expression of praise or regard, as in: *My compliments to the chef.*

comprehensible or comprehensive

Note the different meanings of these words.

○ *comprehensible* means 'capable of being understood', as in: *His teeth were chattering so much that his speech was barely comprehensible.*

○ *comprehensive* means 'including everything that it is possible to include', as in: *The Chancellor has ordered a comprehensive review of departmental spending.*

comprise or compose or constitute or include

These words have related meanings but distinct usages.

○ *comprise* is used for the parts that make up a whole, and for the whole, as in: *The three countries that comprise Great Britain are England, Scotland and Wales.* □ *Great Britain comprises England, Scotland and Wales.* Note that in formal English is it unacceptable to use *comprise* in the passive, eg:

✗ *Great Britain is comprised of England, Scotland and Wales.*

○ *compose* is used of all the parts that make up a whole, as in: *The three countries that compose Great Britain are England, Scotland and Wales.* □ *Great Britain is composed of three countries — England, Scotland and Wales.*

○ *constitute* is used of the elements that added together make something up, but the implication differs from *compose*, in that the elements are not mixed or do not form a new substance or entity, as in: *A balanced diet and regular exercise constitute a healthy lifestyle.*

○ *include* is used of only some of the parts that make up a whole, and should therefore not be confused with *comprise*.

conceit and conceited

The *e* comes before the *i*.

concerto

There are two plurals: **concertos** and **concerti**.

confident or confidant

Be careful not to misspell these words, which have different meanings.

○ A *confidant* is someone in whom one confides, as in: *She has no close confidant to whom she can turn for advice or help.*

○ *confident* means 'having a strong belief in one's abilities, assured', as in: *She was confident she would win.*

connoisseur

Many people misspell this word. Notice the double *n*, the *o* followed by *i*, the double *s*, and the *-eur* ending.

conscience, conscientious and conscious

Remember the *-sci-* combination in the middle of these words.

contagious. See **infectious**.

contemporary

Notice the spelling of the ending. Don't be misled by the way this is often pronounced /-priri/.

contiguous. See **adjacent**.

continual or **continuous**

Do not confuse these words.

○ *continual* means 'constantly repeated or very frequent', as in: *How can I be expected to concentrate when there are continual interruptions?*

○ *continuous* means 'never stopping', as in: *We've had three weeks of continuous rain.*

contrary

Notice the different pronunciations for the different senses.

○ When pronounced /**kon**-tra-ri/ it means 'opposite', as in: *This is contrary to everything we had been hoping to achieve.*

○ When pronounced /kon-**tray**-ri/ it means 'perverse', as in: *She's a contrary little devil.*

controversial and **controversy**

Take care to spell the adjective with *-tro-* (not *-tra-*).

convalescence and **convalescent**

Note the *-val-*, the *-sc-* and the *-ence* and *-ent* endings.

coronary

Note the ending is *-ary* (not *-ory*).

corps

Note that the singular and plural have the same spelling, but the singular is pronounced /kaw(r)/ and the plural /kawr(z)/.

correspondence and **correspondent**

Spelt with double *r* and endings *-ence* and *-ent*.

could or **might**

To avoid any ambiguity *could* should be used to indicate permission, as in: *Mum said we could* (not *might*) *go to the football match. Might* should be used to indicate possibility, as in: *If we hurry we might miss the worst of the traffic.*

➤ See also **can**.

council or counsel

Take care not to confuse these words.

- A *council* is a group of people who organize, control, take decisions or advise.

- *counsel* is a rather formal word meaning 'advice'. It also means 'a lawyer or lawyers'.

councillor or counsellor

- A *councillor* is an elected member of a council.

- A *counsellor* is someone who gives advice.

counterfeit

Remember the *e* comes before the *i*.

courage and courageous

Notice that the *e* of *courage* is not dropped in the adjective *courageous*.

courteous and courtesy

Both words are pronounced /kurt-/, but remember the spelling is -*ou*-. Notice also the *e* in *courteous*, and the -*esy* ending of *courtesy*.

court-martial

There are two plurals: **courts-martial** and **court-martials**. Some people consider the second to be incorrect, though it is generally accepted in informal English.

coxswain

Usually pronounced /**kok**-sun/.

credible or creditable

These words are sometimes confused.

- *credible* means 'believable, likely', as in: *He's the only one without a credible alibi.*

- *creditable* means 'worthy of praise or respect', as in: *For a beginner, he gave a very creditable performance.*

crematorium

There are two possible plurals: **crematoria** and **crematoriums**.

crisis

The plural is **crises**.

criterion

The plural is **criteria**. Take care to avoid the very common error of using the plural form with a singular verb, eg:

> ✗ *The <u>criteria</u> for inclusion in the guide <u>is</u> an exceptionally high standard of service.*
> ✓ *The <u>criterion</u> for inclusion in the guide <u>is</u> an exceptionally high standard of service.*
> ✗ *My <u>criteria</u> for an enjoyable day out <u>is</u> good weather, good company, and no kids!*
> ✓ *My <u>criteria</u> for an enjoyable day <u>are</u> good weather, good company, and no kids!*

critically

Notice the ending is *-ally* (not *-ly*).

crochet

Pronounced /-shay/, but spelt *-chet*.

crooked

Pronounced with two syllables /**kroo**-kid/.

cruel

Notice that in BrE the *l* is doubled in **crueller** and **cruellest**, but in AmE the spellings are **crueler** and **cruelest**.

cryptic

Spelt with *y* (not *i*).

-ction or -xion

Notice the following points relating to these endings.

○ Most words have the ending *-ction*, eg: *action, collection, conjunction, conviction, distinction, extinction, inspection, instruction, production, protection, satisfaction, section.*

○ In BrE (but not in AmE), certain words can be spelt with either ending, eg: *connection/connexion, deflection/deflexion, flection/flexion, genuflection/genuflexion, inflection/inflexion, reflection/reflexion, retroflection/retroflexion.* For these words, the *-ction* ending is commoner, except for *flexion*, *genuflexion* and (in scientific usage) *reflexion*.

○ Certain words must be spelt with the *-xion* ending. They are: *complexion, crucifixion, fluxion* and *transfixion*.

cul-de-sac

The plural is **culs-de-sac**.

curb or **kerb**

Note that in BrE the edge of a pavement is a ***kerb***; in AmE, the edge of a sidewalk is a ***curb***.

currant or **current**

Take care not to confuse the spellings of these words.

○ A ***currant*** is a dried fruit.

○ When ***current*** is a noun it means 'flow', as in: *The current carried the boat out to sea.* □ *an electric current.* As an adjective, ***current*** describes things that are happening now: *What's the current cost of a TV licence?* □ *current affairs.*

curriculum

Remember the double *r*, single *c* and single *l*.

cylinder and **cylindrical**

Spelt *cy-* (not *ci-* or *si-*).

D

dairy or diary

A quick way of remembering whether the spelling is *-ai-* or *-ia-* is to think of the phrase 'the milk is A1 from this dairy'.

dangling participle

The rule in English is that a subordinate clause with no subject of its own should modify the subject of the main clause that it precedes, as in: *Moving like a panther, he crept towards the enemy's camp.* [= 'He' was moving like a panther.]

When a sentence is constructed so that the subordinate clause does not modify the subject of the main clause, the resulting error is known as a ***dangling participle*** (also called a ***misrelated participle***). While listeners usually interpret correctly what is meant in such constructions, dangling participles should nonetheless be avoided in formal and written English. The following are examples, with suggestions for ways to rephrase each sentence:

> ✗ *Growing at two or three feet a week, the other plants are in danger of being smothered by that vine.* [Was it the vine or the other plants that is/are growing so quickly?]
>
> ✓ *The other plants are in danger of being smothered by that vine, which is growing at two or three feet a week.*
>
> ✗ *While sitting on the lavatory, a red-backed spider bit him.* [Was the man or the spider sitting on the lavatory?]
>
> ✓ *While he was sitting on the lavatory, a red-backed spider bit him.*

data

Strictly speaking, **data** is a plural noun (with singular **datum**), and thus should be followed by a plural verb, as in: *The data in this report <u>were</u> assembled over a period of several years.* However, it is now commonplace to find ***data*** used as a mass (or collective) noun followed by a singular verb, as in: *The data in this report <u>was</u> assembled over a period of years.*

decide, decided or decisive

Remember that these words are spelt with *de* and *c*.

defective or deficient

These adjectives are sometimes confused.

○ *defective* means 'having a fault or flaw', as in: *The company has recalled all the cars suspected of having defective gear boxes.*

○ *deficient* means 'lacking in what is needed, inadequate', as in: *A diet of junk food is deficient in essential vitamins and minerals.*

defer and deferral

Notice that the *r* in *defer* is doubled in the noun *deferral* and in the verb forms **deferring** and **deferred**.

definite or definitive

These words have different meanings. Note also the spellings, with *-nit-* (not *-nat-*).

○ *definite* means 'certain' or 'clear, not vague', as in: *I can't give you a definite answer until next week.*

○ *definitive* means 'authoritative, that cannot be improved upon', as in: *This is regarded as the definitive work on language development in young children.*

defuse or diffuse

The spellings of these words are sometimes confused.

○ *defuse* is a verb and is pronounced /dee-**fewz**/. Its literal meaning is 'to remove the fuse from (a bomb)'. It also means 'to make (a situation) less tense'.

○ *diffuse* as a verb is pronounced /di-**fewz**/ and means 'to spread in all directions'. As an adjective it is pronounced /di-**fews**/.

delusion. See illusion.

deny. See refute.

dependant or dependent

Take care to use the correct spellings.

○ *dependant* is a noun and means 'a person who depends on another for money, food, etc', as in: *As a young man without dependants, he was free to spend his money as he pleased.*

○ *dependent* is an adjective, as in: *He's still dependent on state benefit.* □ *a clinic where drug- and alcohol-dependent celebrities go for treatment.*

deprecate or depreciate

These words are easy to confuse, especially because derivatives of ***deprecate*** are often used in the sense of 'belittling', as in: *He uses self-deprecation as a sort of defence against criticism.*

○ ***deprecate*** means 'to express disapproval of', as in: *She wrote to him in forthright terms, deprecating his irresponsibility.*

○ ***depreciate*** means 'to fall in value', as in: *New cars depreciate by as much as 25% in the first year*. It also means 'to belittle', as in: *He felt that all he had achieved was being depreciated by jealous and ambitious newcomers.*

derisive or derisory

In the past, these words were synonymous. Now however, their meanings differ, as follows:

○ ***derisive*** means 'mocking, showing derision', as in: *derisive laughter.*

○ ***derisory*** means 'deserving derision or mockery, ridiculous', as in: *He earned the derisory sum of £5 for ten hours' work.*

desert or dessert

Because their spellings are so similar, it is quite easy to misspell these words. A quick way of remembering which is which is to think of '<u>s</u>ugar and <u>s</u>pice', often found in a de<u>ss</u>ert.

despatch. See dispatch.

detach and attach

Remember: there is no *t* before the *ch* in these words.

deteriorate

Pronounced with five distinct syllables /di-**teer**-ee-i-rayt/.

develop and development

There is no *e* at the end of ***develop***, or between the *p* and the *m* of ***development***. The *p* in ***develop*** is not doubled in the verb forms **developing** and **developed**.

dial

In BrE, the *l* is doubled in the verb forms **dialling** and **dialled**. In AmE, the spellings are **dialing** and **dialed**.

diaphragm

Spelt with *ph* (not *f*), and notice the *g*.

diarrhoea

Notice the *-rrh-* combination (from ancient Greek *rheein* = to flow). In AmE, the spelling is **diarrhea**.

diary. See **dairy**.

dice or **die**

    Die is the singular of *dice*, but is now rarely used except in the phrase 'the die is cast'. *Dice* is used as both the singular and the plural: *The dice is/are in that box*.

differ from or **differ with**

  ○ *differ from* means 'to be different from', as in: *Her approach differs from mine in that it is a little more subtle*.

  ○ *differ with* means 'to disagree with', as in: *I differ with her over how to deal with disruptive children*.

different from or **different than** or **different to**

    It is perfectly acceptable in BrE to follow *different* with either **from** or **to**, eg: *That car is different from the one he had yesterday.* ❑ *Is that car different to the one you had yesterday?* Some people prefer to use *different from* for written English, but both are correct. In AmE, *different than* is commonly used, but it is less acceptable in BrE and should therefore be avoided in formal speech and writing, except in instances where *different* is followed by a clause rather than a noun or pronoun, eg: *It was a different car he arrived in this morning than the one he had yesterday*.

diffuse. See **defuse**.

dilemma

    Spelt with single *l* and double *m*. A *dilemma* is a difficult choice between two (or more) equally unfavourable alternatives, as in: *He was faced with the dilemma of risking war with one of his neighbours or disappointing the other*. It is not acceptable in standard English to use *dilemma* to mean simply 'a problem', where there is no element of choice involved, eg:

    ✗ *His dilemma is that he has no money*.

dinghy or **dingy**

    Do not confuse the spellings of these words. Note also that *dinghy* is pronounced /**ding**-gi/ with a hard *g* and *dingy* is pronounced /**din**-ji/ with a soft *g*.

  ○ A *dinghy* is a small boat.

  ○ *dingy* is an adjective meaning 'dark and dirty', as in: *The disco was held in a dingy basement*.

diphtheria and diphthong

Spelt with *ph* followed by *th*. The **ph** combination should be pronounced *f* (not *p*), hence /dif-**theer**-i-a/ and /**dif**-thong/.

disastrous

Pronounced /di-**sas**-trus/ (not /di-**sas**-ter-us/).

disc or disk

In AmE, spelt with a *k* for any flat circular object. In BrE, only computer disks are spelt with a *k*.

discreet or discrete

These are different words with different meanings.

○ *discreet* means 'not saying or doing anything that may cause trouble or embarrassment', as in: *This is a very delicate matter: can we rely on you to be discreet?*

○ *discrete* means 'separate, not connected or attached to others', as in: *On closer examination, we find that the pattern is formed from thousands of discrete dots of colour.*

disinterested. See uninterested.

dispatch or despatch

Both spellings are correct, but the one with *e* is less common. Notice the *t* before the *ch*.

distinct or distinctive

Notice the difference in the meanings of these words.

○ *distinct* means 'clearly or easily seen, heard, etc', as in: *a distinct smell of alcohol on his breath.*

○ *distinctive* means 'characteristic', as in: *the distinctive call of the peewit* ▫ *He has a distinctive walk.*

do

When we talk, we often use *do* to avoid repeating a verb, as in: *You make better lasagne than I do.* ▫ *He beckoned to the waitress to come over, and she did.*

There are certain constructions in which this use of *do* is not correct, and these should be avoided, especially in formal and written English.

○ Leave out *do* after **used to** and when (as the present participle *doing*) it follows the verb *to be*, eg:

✗ *I don't play golf as much as I used to do.*

✓ *I don't play golf as much as I used to.*

✗ 'Is he working on the car?' 'He was doing, but he might have stopped for a coffee.'

✓ 'Is he working on the car?' 'He was, but he might have stopped for a coffee.'

○ **do** should not be used to replace the verb *to be*, eg:

✗ *He told me to be careful but I didn't.*

✓ *He told me to be careful but I wasn't.*

○ Take care not to mix the active and passive voice. **Do** and the verb it is replacing should agree, eg:

✗ *Charlie's mistake was joked about by the lads today in the same way as they did yesterday.*

✓ *The lads joked about Charlie's mistake today in the same way as they did yesterday.*

○ **do** should not be used to replace **have**:

✗ *He has more courage than I do.*

✓ *He has more courage than I have.*

doesn't or don't

Remember that it is incorrect to use **don't** for the third person present singular of the verb **do**, as in:

✗ *It don't seem fair.*

✓ *It doesn't seem fair.*

double comparatives

Take care to avoid the mistake of applying two comparatives to the same word, as in:

✗ *It's much more colder than it was yesterday.*

✗ *She's a more happier child since she changed schools.*

Say instead:

✓ *It's much colder than it was yesterday.*

✓ *She's a happier child since she changed schools.*

double negatives

In non-standard forms of English **double negatives** are often used for emphasis. For example, '*He didn't say nothing,*' means the same as '*He didn't say anything at all*'.

However, in standard English it is considered to be bad style to have two negatives in the same simple sentence or clause, because the second negative has the effect of cancelling out the first.

✗ *I don't want no trouble.*

✓ *I don't want any trouble.*

Words which have the meaning 'nearly not' (*hardly*, *barely* and *scarcely*) should also be treated as negatives.

  ✗ *He was so drunk he couldn't hardly stand.*

  ✓ *He was so drunk he could hardly stand.*

Take care not to add a negative that would change the intended meaning, as in: *I wouldn't be at all surprised if it didn't snow tonight.* If you mean that it is very likely to snow tonight, this should be: *I wouldn't be at all surprised if it snowed tonight.*

downward or downwards

Downward can be an adverb or an adjective. *Downwards* is only an adverb. In BrE the more usual adverb is *downwards*, while in AmE it is *downward*, as in: (BrE) *They slid downwards.* □ (AmE) *They slid downward.*

draft or draught

In BrE only the senses 'a rough sketch or outline' and 'an order from or to a bank for the payment of money' have the *-ft* spelling. All other senses in BrE are spelt with *-ught*. In AmE, all senses are spelt with *-ft*.

drier or dryer

The adjective meaning 'more dry' is spelt with *i*. The noun meaning 'a machine for drying' can be spelt with *i* or *y*.

duel or dual

Do not confuse the spellings of these words.

○ A *duel* is a fight with swords or pistols.

○ *dual* is an adjective meaning 'double', as in: *He has dual citizenship* [= he is a citizen of two countries].

duly or dully

Because they are so alike, these words are often misspelled.

○ *duly* means 'properly, as expected', as in: *He was duly punished.* Notice there is no *e* in *duly*, although it derives from **due**.

○ *dully* means 'in a dull way', as in: *A few stars shone dully through the thickening smog.*

dyeing or dying

Dyeing is the present participle of **dye** [= to colour with dye]. *Dying* is the present participle of **die** [= to stop living].

due to. See because of.

E

each

- ○ Use a plural verb when *each* follows a plural noun or pronoun, as in: *The children each <u>have</u> a PC of their own.* □ *They each <u>have</u> a PC of their own.*
- ○ Use a singular verb when *each* is the subject of the sentence or clause, as in: *There are twenty houses in the terrace. Each* (house) <u>has</u> *its own back and front garden.*
- ○ Use a singular verb with *each of* followed by a plural noun (that is, where *each* is part of the subject of the sentence or clause), as in: *Each of these houses <u>has</u> its own front and back garden.* It is also acceptable to use a plural verb when you want to avoid using '*his or her*' to refer back to a plural noun, eg:
  - ✓ *Each of the directors <u>has</u> his or her own parking space.*
  - ✓ *Each of the directors <u>have</u> their own parking space.*

each other or one another

The convention is that these phrases should not be used interchangeably: *each other* should only be used to refer to two people, and *one another* should only be used to refer to more than two, as in: *The two farmers helped each other at harvest time.* □ *All the farmers in the area helped one another at harvest time.* However, in modern usage it is quite acceptable to treat these two phrases as grammatical equivalents, as in: *All the farmers in the area helped each other at harvest time.* □ *The two farmers helped one another at harvest time.*

earring

Remember: this word is formed from the words *ear* and *ring*, and is therefore spelt with double *r*.

eatable or edible

When the meaning is simply 'that may be eaten', these two words can be used synonymously, as in: *The toast was burnt and barely eatable/edible*. There is nonetheless a difference in meaning, which in other contexts can be extremely important. If something is **eatable**, it may be eaten (though it may not be safe or desirable to do so); but, if something is **edible** it is safe to eat. For example, the pods of the laburnum tree may look **eatable** but are extremely poisonous; and, while it may be rather unusual to eat flowers, nasturtiums and courgette flowers are **edible**.

eccentric and eccentricity

Remember: these words are spelt *ecc-* (not *exc-*).

ecstatic and ecstacy

Remember: these words are spelt *ecs-* (not *exs-*). Notice also the ending of **ecstacy** is *-acy* (not *-asy*).

economic or economical

These words should not be confused.

○ **economic** means 'relating to economics, the study of money' or 'giving a reasonable profit', as in: *an economic survey of Scotland □ Without generous subsidies, many smaller farms just wouldn't be economic.*

○ **economical** means 'careful with money or other resources, not wasteful', as in: *He's had to learn to be more economical now that his only income is a small pension.*

eczema

The skin condition is pronounced /**ex**-si-ma/ and spelt *ecze-*.

edible. See eatable.

eerie, eerily, and eeriness

These words start with double *e*. Notice also that the last *e* in **eerie** is dropped when the endings *-ily* and *-iness* are added.

effect. See affect.

effective or effectual

Although there is a broad overlap in meaning between these words, each has distinct senses which ought to affect the choice of which one to use.

○ **effective** means 'successful, likely to be successful', as in: *The only effective way of maintaining a weed-free border is to cover the soil with black polythene or old carpet*. It also means 'impressive, powerful', as in: *Despite his small stature, Mussolini was an effective speaker*. A further sense refers to something, such as a law, coming into operation or force, as in: *a new tax allowance, effective from January 2000*. Finally, **effective** means 'in reality, even if not in name or in theory', as in: *The old king is very frail. His eldest son is now the effective ruler, though he hasn't yet been appointed regent.*

○ **effectual** means 'actually successful', as in: *The measures introduced by the last government to control welfare spending proved to be effectual in some areas but not in others.*

➤ See also **efficient** below.

efficient and efficacious

These adjectives come from the same Latin word *efficere*, from the Latin prefix *ex* out + *facere* to make. In modern English, both words refer to the result or effect of something, but their usage differs.

○ **efficient** is mostly applied to the way in which a result is achieved, rather than the result itself. It means 'producing a result or getting things done in a competent way, without wasting time, effort, money, etc', as in: *My personal assistant is so efficient, I never have to worry about the day-to-day running of the office.* □ *Covering the soil with old carpet is a cost-efficient method of eradicating weeds in the newly-dug border.*

○ **efficacious** is a formal word meaning 'producing the intended or necessary result'. It is nowadays only applied to medicine or medical treatment that produces a cure, as in: *Snake oil, only a dollar a bottle, an efficacious remedy for all manner of ailments.*

egoist or egotist

Both these words are used to mean 'a self-centred person', though strictly speaking there is a useful distinction between them that is worth maintaining.

○ An **egoist** is a person whose selfishness is based on the philosophical principle that the only certainty is one's own existence, and self-interest is thus a legitimate basis for morality.

○ An **egotist** is a person who is self-important and vain, and talks about themselves a great deal.

-ei-. See **-ie-**.

eight and eighth

Notice there is only one *t* in **eighth**, unlike other ordinals where

47

th is added to the end of the cardinal number, as in *sixth, seventh, tenth, fourteenth,* etc.

either

The *ei-* may be pronounced /iy-/ or /ee-/. Both are acceptable. Note the following points relating to the use of *either* in sentence construction.

○ When *either* is a pronoun it can only be used to refer to two people or things, as in: *There are two alternatives. Either of them is practicable.* If there are more than two people or things, remember to use **any** instead, as in: *There were dozens of applicants, but I don't think any of them was suitable.* In these examples, notice that a singular rather than a plural verb is used because *either* and **any** are part of the subject of the clause.

○ When *either* is followed by **or** and the two noun or noun-phrase subjects it links are singular, the verb is singular, as in: *Either Rosie or Bill <u>is</u> right.* If the second of the linked subjects is plural, the verb is also plural, as in: *If either Rosie or her sisters <u>are</u> not telling the truth, we'll soon know.* When both of the linked subjects are plural, the verb is plural, as in: *You tend to find that either teenage children or elderly parents <u>are</u> making demands on your time.*

○ To avoid ambiguity, take care to place **either** as close as possible to the items it refers to, eg:

✗ *I intend to either phone them today or on Monday.*
✓ *I intend to phone them either today or on Monday.*

elder and eldest

Elder and *eldest* can only be used when referring to the relative age of the members of a family, and the adjective is preceded by its noun or a determiner such as *the, my,* or *his.* In all other instances, use **older** or **oldest** instead.

✓ *This is my elder brother, John.*
✓ *My brother Peter is the eldest.*
✗ *Carbon-dating shows that this is the elder of the two skeletons.*
✓ *Carbon-dating shows that this is the older of the two skeletons.*
✗ *Peter is eldest.*
✓ *Peter is oldest.*

elude. See allude.

embarrass and **embarrassment**

Notice the double *r* and double *s*. Omission of the second *r* is a frequent error.

emend. See **amend**.

enforce and **enforceable**

Notice that the *e* in *enforce* is not dropped in the adjective *enforceable*.

English, Scottish and **Welsh**

People from other parts of the world often refer to anyone from Great Britain as *English*. Only people from England are *English*. People from Scotland are *Scottish* and people from Wales are *Welsh*. However, it is correct to refer to people from all three countries as **British**.

enormity or **enormousness**

Take care to use *enormousness* rather than *enormity* for large size, as in: *the enormousness of the stadium*. *Enormity* denotes extreme wickedness or a very serious mistake, as in: *shocked by the enormity of their crimes* □ *Only then did she realise the enormity of her error*.

enrol or **enroll**

Remember: single *l* in BrE and double *l* in AmE. However, in both BrE and AmE the *l* is doubled in **enrolling** and **enrolled**.

envelop or **envelope**

Note the different spellings and pronunciations for the different parts of speech.

○ *envelop* is the verb, meaning 'to completely surround or cover' and is pronounced /en-**vel**-up/.

○ *envelope* is the noun, and is pronounced /**en**-vel-ope/.

equable or **equitable**

These words are sometimes confused.

○ *equable* means 'without extremes, moderate', as in: *Britain has an equable climate*. It also means 'even-tempered', as in: *That child would drive even the most equable parent mad*.

○ *equitable* means 'fair, just', as in: *Lawyers for both partners are satisfied that the divorce settlement is equitable*.

equal

Remember: the *l* is doubled in the verb forms **equalling** and **equalled**.

equally

Do not use **as** after *equally*, eg:

   ✗ *This sparkling wine is equally as good as champagne.*
   ✓ *This sparkling wine is as good as champagne.*

-er, -or or -ar

It is easy to misspell words with these endings.

○ *-er* is used to form nouns that mean someone or something that performs the action of a verb: that is, so-called 'doer' nouns. Note that this is the ending generally used when new nouns are formed from verbs. The following list is of some *-er* words formed from core verbs.

announcer	dancer	opener	talker
builder	doer	plasterer	teacher
buyer	knocker	racer	trailer
cooker	lecturer	singer	worker
cruiser	mixer	surfer	

○ *-er* is also used to form some nouns based on or related to other nouns or adjectives.

foreigner	lawyer	prisoner	treasurer
jeweller	mariner	sorcerer	usurer

○ *-or* is also used to form many 'doer' nouns. The following list contains some of the commonest.

accelerator	counsellor	inheritor	professor
actor	creator	inspector	projector
administrator	decorator	inventor	protector
arbitrator	dictator	investigator	radiator
auditor	director	investor	refrigerator
calculator	distributor	legislator	sailor
collector	duplicator	mediator	spectator
commentator	editor	narrator	supervisor
competitor	educator	navigator	surveyor
conductor	elevator	objector	survivor
conqueror	escalator	operator	translator
conspirator	excavator	oppressor	vendor
contractor	governor	orator	ventilator
contributor	incubator	perpetrator	visitor
councillor	indicator	processor	

○ **-or** is also used for certain other nouns.

ambassador	creditor	janitor	solicitor
ancestor	curator	major	sponsor
author	debtor	mayor	successor
aviator	doctor	pastor	suitor
bachelor	emperor	predecessor	tailor
benefactor	equator	proctor	tenor
captor	impostor	proprietor	tractor
censor	inquisitor	rector	traitor
chancellor	jailor	senator	victor

○ A small number of adjectives end in **-or**.

anterior	interior	posterior	tenor
exterior	major	superior	ulterior
inferior	minor		

○ **-ar** is also used in a small number of 'doer' nouns, and for certain other common nouns.

altar	cedar	hangar	pillar
beggar	cellar	liar	registrar
burglar	collar	molar	scholar
bursar	dollar	mortar	vicar
calendar	grammar	nectar	vinegar
caterpillar	guitar	pedlar	

○ There are a number of adjectives ending in **-ar**.

angular	lunar	perpendicular	singular
circular	molecular	polar	spectacular
familiar	muscular	popular	stellar
insular	particular	regular	tubular
jocular	peculiar	similar	vulgar

especially. See **specially**.

etc

A common error is to write *ect*. Think of the full form *et cetera* for the correct order of the last two letters of the abbreviation.

evade. See **avert**.

even

When writing, take care to place **even** in the correct position in the sentence. This is not so important for spoken English because you can use the inflection of your voice to emphasize parts of the sentence so that your meaning is clearly understood. To avoid ambiguity in writing, the adverb **even** should go immediately before the word being emphasized. Notice the effect that putting it in different places has on the meaning in the following examples:

Even I had washed the floor. [= It was unusual for me to wash the floor.]

I had even washed the floor. [= I had washed the floor as well as sweeping it.]

I had washed even the floor. [= I had washed everything including the floor.]

every

Note that when **every** is part of a noun phrase it is followed by a singular verb, as in: *Every other house <u>has</u> broken windows or graffiti on the walls.*

everyone and every one

In writing, take care to use the correct form.

○ **everyone** means 'every person in a group' or 'all people in general', as in: *Everyone we'd invited came to the party.* □ *Everyone seems to know someone who has lost his or her job recently.*

○ **every one** means 'all the people or things mentioned', as in: *Every one of the houses in the new estate has been sold.*

evoke or invoke

These words share the meaning 'to call up' but their specific meanings extend this sense so that there is a distinction between them.

○ **evoke** means 'to cause or produce' or 'to bring into the mind', as in: *The withdrawal of financial support evoked an angry response from community leaders.* □ *The scent of lavender evoked memories of winters spent at her grandmother's house while her parents toured the provinces.*

○ **invoke** means 'to call up a spirit' or 'to use or bring into operation', as in: *The shaman invokes the spirits of their ancestors.* □ *When challenged about the benefits of treatment in such cases, doctors often invoke their sworn duty to preserve life.* □ *If our case fails in the national courts we will invoke the European Declaration on Human Rights.*

exaggerate

Commonly misspelled. Remember: double *g* and single *r*.

excerpt

When writing this word, don't be misled by the pronunciation /**ex**-sert/.

exceed

Spelt with *ex-* followed by c and double *e*.

➤ Compare **accede**.

excise

This word is pronounced in the same way as *size*, but it is spelt *-cise*. It cannot be spelt *-ize*.

exercise

Never spell the ending of this word *-ize*.

exhaust and **exhaustion**

Remember the *h* followed by *-au-* in these words.

exhibit and **exhibition**

Don't forget the *h* in these words, usually not sounded when spoken.

extraordinary

In writing, take care not to miss out the first *a*, which is often not sounded when spoken.

extravert or **extrovert**

Both spellings are correct.

F

faint or feint

Take care not to confuse the spellings of these words, which have the same pronunciation.

○ To *faint* means to lose consciousness suddenly.

○ A *feint* is a move intended to deceive an opponent.

farther. See further.

fascination

It is quite common for people to say that 'they have a fascination for something', when they are fascinated by that thing. This is not considered to be standard English. The correct construction is 'something has a fascination for them'.

✗ *Most young babies have a fascination for brightly-coloured moving objects.*

✓ *Brightly-coloured moving objects have a fascination for most young babies.*

fatal or fateful

Do not confuse these words.

○ *fatal* means 'causing death or disaster' or (in formal or literary usage) 'chosen or appointed by fate', as in: *a fatal accident* ▫ *He made a fatal mistake.* ▫ *At that fatal hour, they will meet again.* ▫ *Alone he rides, alone, the fair and fatal king.*

○ *fateful* means 'crucial, significant, deciding one's fate', as in: *On that one fateful day in October, millions of pounds were wiped off the value of shares.*

feasible

Spelling: note the *-eas-* and the *-ible* ending.

Feasible comes from the French word *faisable* meaning 'that can be done'. In informal English, it is sometimes used as a synonym for 'likely' or 'possible' (effectively omitting the 'done' part of the literal meaning). This is regarded as non-standard usage and should be avoided in formal English.

> ✓ *Would tell me if you think my plan is feasible* [= can be done].
> ✗ *I suppose it is feasible that the plane might crash.*

February

If you have trouble remembering the correct spelling, try to ignore the commonest pronunciations /**feb**-ra-ri/ and /**feb**-ya-ri/ and think only of the pronunciation /**feb**-roo-a-ri/. This will help to remind you that there is a *u* before the *-ary*.

feint. See **faint**.

fewer or less

Take care not to use *fewer* when you should use *less*, and vice versa.

○ *fewer* is used with plural countable nouns, eg: *There are fewer fruits on the apple tree this year.* □ *If fewer people smoked there would be fewer cases of heart disease.* □ *He has fewer stresses in his life nowadays.* □ *I might not be so fat if I ate fewer cakes and chocolates.* □ *There were fewer than 20 people at the meeting.*

○ *less* is used with uncountable nouns, eg: *There is less fruit on the apple tree this year.* □ *If fewer people smoked there would be less heart disease.* □ *He has less stress in his life nowadays.* □ *I might not be so fat if I ate fewer cakes and less chocolate.*

○ *less* is also used for specific amounts of money, eg: *He earns less than twelve thousand pounds a year.* It is also preferred for other specific quantities, eg: *He lives less than three miles away.* □ *We have twenty-four hours or less to reach the injured climber.*

fictional and fictitious

While these words share the broad meaning 'invented, not real', their specific senses are distinct.

○ *fictional* denotes imaginary people or things created for stories: *Ian Fleming's fictional hero, James Bond, is said to be based on a real person.*

○ *fictitious* denotes something that is not real and has been created with the intention of deceiving others: *He gave the police a fictitious name.*

fidget

Note that the verb forms **fidgeting** and **fidgeted** have only one *t*.

field, fiend and **fierce**

The *i* comes before the *e* in all these words.

fiery

This adjective means 'like fire', but note there is an *e* after the *i*.

flammable. See **inflammable**.

flaunt or **flout**

The meanings of these words are sometimes confused.

○ *flaunt* means 'to show (something) off in an ostentatious way', as in: *You've got a good figure, and as the saying goes, 'If you've got it, flaunt it!'*

○ *flout* means 'to refuse to obey or comply with', as in: *He seems to take pleasure in flouting the law.*

focus

The noun has two plurals: **focuses** (in general usage) and **foci** (in scientific and technical usage). The verb forms can be spelt **focuses** or **focusses**, **focusing** or **focussing**, and **focused** or **focussed**.

forbid

The past tense is **forbade** (pronounced /for-**bad**/ or /for-**bade**/), and the past participle is **forbidden**. Also note that the *d* is doubled in **forbidding** and **forbidden**.

forceps

Note that *forceps* takes a plural verb, as in: *These forceps <u>are</u> used to help deliver babies.* However, 'a pair of *forceps*' takes a singular verb, as in: *<u>Has</u> this pair of forceps been sterilized?*

foreign and **foreigner**

Remember: these words are exceptions to the '*i* before *e*, except after *c*' rule. The *e* comes before the *i*.

forgive and **forgivable**

Notice that the *e* of *forgive* is dropped when adding the -*able* ending.

➤ Compare **giveable**.

formula

There are two plurals: **formulas** (in general use) and **formulae** (in scientific and technical use).

forty

Remember: there is no *u* in *forty*.

frolic

Notice that *k* is added in the verb forms **frolicking** and **frolicked**.

fulfil or fulfill and fulfilment or fulfillment

These words are frequently misspelled. In particular, note the *l* before the second *f*.

The BrE spelling has a single *l* at the end of *fulfil* and in the middle of *fulfilment*, while in AmE, in both cases, the *l* is doubled. Notice, however, in BrE the *l* is doubled in **fulfilling** and **fulfilled**.

funnel

In BrE, the *l* is doubled in **funnelling** and **funnelled**. In AmE, the spellings are **funneling** and **funneled**.

furore

Pronounced with three syllables, with the stress on the second syllable /fyoo-**raw**-rei/.

further or farther

The adjective and adverb *further* can be used for all senses, eg: *How much further is it to Aberdeen?* □ *I want to make one further point before we finish our discussion*. It can only be replaced by *farther* when physical distance is involved, eg:

✓ *How much farther is it to Aberdeen?*

✗ *I want to make one farther point before we finish our discussion.*

fused participle

A *fused participle* is a structure in which an *-ing* word is preceded by a non-possessive noun or pronoun, as in: *Bill leaving without saying goodbye surprised us all.* □ *We were surprised at him going like that*. This is still regarded by some as non-standard usage. According to the traditional rule, the noun or pronoun should be in the possessive form: *Bill's leaving without saying goodbye surprised us all.* □ *We were surprised at his going like that*. However, this rule is no longer generally adhered to, and indeed the 'correct' form often seems overly formal in modern usage.

G

gallop
Remember: single *p* in **galloping** and **galloped**.

gamble or gambol
These words have different meanings.

○ To **gamble** means 'to bet', as in: *He sometimes gambles at the casino*.

○ To **gambol** means 'to jump and skip playfully', as in: *There were a couple of puppies gambolling in the yard*. Notice that in BrE the *l* is doubled in **gambolling** and **gambolled**: in AmE the spellings are **gamboling** and **gamboled**.

gaol and jail
Note that **gaol** is a variant spelling of **jail** and is pronounced /jayl/, not /gohl/.

gauge
Pronounced /gayj/ and spelt -*au*- (not -*ua*-).

genetics
Note that **genetics** is followed by a singular verb, as in: *Genetics is his specialism*.

genre
Pronounced /**zhon**-ruh/.

gents and ladies
When the meaning is 'a lavatory (for men or for women)', both these words take a singular verb, as in: *Where is the gents?* □ *The ladies is at the end of the hall*.

get
The present participle is **getting** and the past participle is **got**. In AmE, the past participle **gotten** is also used, as in: *They have gotten permission from their parents*.
Note that it is better to avoid certain common informal uses of

get and *got* in formal written English. These are:

○ the use of *get* to form the passive, eg:
  ✗ *Do not put a baby into a hot bath. It might get scalded.*

○ the use of *have got* for 'have', and *have got to* for 'must', eg:
  ✗ *I have got the mumps.*   ✗ *I have got to finish this report.*

○ the use of *get* or *got* instead of a more explicit verb, eg:
  ✗ *I got there in the evening.*
  ✓ *I arrived there in the evening.*
  ✗ *He got a bottle of wine for the party.*
  ✓ *He bought a bottle of wine for the party.*
  ✗ *I expect to get your cheque this week.*
  ✓ *I expect to receive your cheque this week.*

ghastly
Notice the *h*, which is not sounded when spoken.

ghetto
Remember the *h* and the double *t*. The plural can be spelt **ghettos** or **ghettoes**.

gild or guild
Notice the different spellings.

○ To *gild* means 'to cover with gold'.

○ A *guild* is an assocation or club.

gipsy. See gypsy.

giraffe
Spelt with double *f*.

givable or giveable
In AmE both forms are correct. Only the form with the *e* is used in BrE.

➤ Compare **forgivable**.

glamour, glamorize, glamorise and glamorous
Notice that the *u* of *glamour* is dropped in *glamorize* and *glamorous*. In AmE, *glamour* may also be spelt *glamor*, and *glamorize* is always spelt with the ending *-ize*.

gonorrhoea
This word is frequently misspelled. Note that in AmE the usual spelling is **gonorrhea**.

good

The use of **good** as a substitute for the adverb **well** is not acceptable in standard English, eg:

   ✗ *He did good in his exams.*
   ✓ *He did well in his exams.*

gorgeous

Take care not to forget the *e*.

got and gotten. See get.

gourmand or gourmet

Notice the different meanings.

○ A **gourmand** is a person who eats a lot, a glutton.

○ A **gourmet** is a person who enjoys, and knows a lot about, good food and wine.

govern and government

Take care to include the *n* in **government**, which is not sounded when spoken. Think of the spelling of **govern** when writing the noun.

graffiti

Spelt with double *f* and single *t*. Note also that **graffiti** is a plural noun and, strictly speaking, should be followed by a plural verb, as in: *The graffiti <u>are</u> removed with a special solvent.* The singular, which is rarely used, is **graffito**.

grammar and grammatical

Remember: **grammar** is spelt with *-ar* (not *-er*). Thinking of the pronunciation of **grammatical** will help to avoid this common error.

grateful, gratefully and gratitude

Notice the *-ate-* in **grateful**, the double *l* in **gratefully**, and the *i* in **gratitude**.

grief, grieve, grievance and grievous

Remember the *i* before the *e*. Note also **grievous** has no *i* following the *v* and is pronounced /**gree**-vis/.

guarantee

Notice the *u* and the single *r*.

guerrilla and guerilla

Spelt with either double or single *r*, and double *l*. Take care not to confuse guerrilla 'a fighter' with **gorilla** 'a large African ape'.

guild. See **gild**.

guilt and **guilty**
Remember the u before the i.

gynaecologist and **gynaecology**
Notice the y. In AmE these words are often spelt without the a.

gypsy and **gipsy**
Both spellings are correct, but the y spelling is more common.

H

haemo- or hemo-

Many words that include the prefix *haemo-* are difficult to spell correctly. Remember that the prefix is always spelt *haemo-* in BrE, but may also be spelt *hemo-* in AmE. Notice the spellings of the following words: haemoglobin, haemophilia, haemophiliac, haemorrhage, haemorrhoid.

half and half of

Note the following points relating to the usage of *half* and *half of*.

○ It is equally acceptable to use *half* or *half of* before a noun, as in: *Half the men went to the pub instead of helping to clear up.* □ *Half of the men went to the pub instead of helping to clear up.*

○ However, *half of* rather than *half* should be used before a pronoun, as in: *Half of them went to the pub.*

○ With quantities and times, use *half* with the indefinite article, eg: *half a dozen* □ *a half dozen* □ *a pound and a half* □ *ten and a half inches* □ *a mile and a half* □ *half an hour* □ *half a day's march.* Take care not to use two indefinite articles with quantities or times, eg:
✗ *a half a day's march.*

○ When *half* or *half of* is used with a singular or uncountable noun, the verb is singular, eg: *Half the garden <u>is</u> submerged.* □ *Half of our furniture <u>is</u> falling to pieces.*

○ When *half* or *half of* is used with a plural countable noun, the verb is plural, eg: *Half the plants in the garden <u>are</u> dead or dying.* □ *More than half of their possessions <u>were</u> lost in the fire.* But, with quantities and times, note that the verb is singular even if the noun is plural, eg: *Ten and a half days <u>is</u> a long time to wait to be rescued.*

handkerchief

When spelling this word, don't be misled by the way it is commonly pronounced. Remember the *d* and the *e* after the *i*.

hangar or hanger

Note the spellings for the different senses.

○ A *hangar* is a large building in which aeroplanes are kept.

○ A *hanger* is used to hang up clothes. This is also the spelling for words like *hanger-on*, etc.

hanged. See hung.

harass and harassment

Notice the single *r* and the double *s*.

➤ Compare **embarrass**.

hardly. See barely.

have

Note the following points relating to the usage of *have*.

○ In BrE, the present perfect tense (that is, with *have*) is usually used with words like **already** or **just**, eg: *I have already showered.* □ *I've just showered.* But, in AmE, the simple past is used: *I already showered.* □ *I just showered.* The AmE usage is becoming increasingly common in BrE.

○ In spoken English, and sometimes in written English too, an extra *have* is sometimes inserted, especially in conditional clauses. This is ungrammatical and must be avoided.

✗ *If he'd (or he had) have done it, his dad would have smacked him.*

✗ *If he had've done it, his dad would have smacked him.*

✓ *If he'd (or he had) done it, his dad would have smacked him.*

✗ *They'd have hated to have seen that happen.*

✓ *They'd hate to have seen that happen.*

✓ *They'd have hated to see that happen.*

headquarters

Headquarters can be followed by a singular or plural verb, as in: *The company headquarters is/are in the States.*

height

Although related to *high* notice the *e*, which comes before the *i*.

63

heinous

Pronounced /**hee**-nus/ or /**hay**-nus/. Notice the *e* comes before the *i*, and that there is no *i* between the *n* and *-ous*.

hemo-. See haemo-.

here and there

With *here* and *there*, the verb should agree with the following noun or pronoun: that is, singular verb with singular noun or pronoun; plural verb with plural noun or pronoun, eg:

✓ Here <u>are</u> Suzanne and Heather.

✗ Here<u>'s</u> Suzanne and Heather.

In informal English, **is** (or more often its short form **'s**) is often used before a plural complement, but this is not acceptable in formal or written English, eg:

✗ There<u>'s</u> many problems we have to solve first.

✓ There <u>are</u> many problems we have to solve first.

However, with quantities considered as a single amount, the singular verb **is** (rather than the plural **are**) is correct, eg: *Here<u>'s</u> seventy pence for your bus fare.*

Note also that the singular verb is correct when you are listing individual people or things that are to be considered separately, eg: *'What shall we have for dinner?' 'Well, there<u>'s</u> chicken and fish in the freezer, and pasta and quiche in the fridge.'*

heroin or heroine

Remember: the form without the *e* at the end is the drug, and the form with the *e* at the end is a woman noted for bravery or who is the subject of a story.

hers

Remember: *hers* does not have an apostrophe.

hiccup or hiccough

Both spellings are correct.

hideous

Spelling: note the *e*.

historic or historical

Note the difference in meaning.

○ *historic* means 'important in history, or likely to be remembered for a long time', as in: *a historic monument* □ *a historic battle*. In recent times, and especially in the sphere of politics, *historic* has been rather overused and the word is in danger of becoming devalued. For this reason, try to avoid phrases like '*a historic agreement*' in writing.

○ ***historical*** means 'of or about (real) people or events in history', as in: *a historical novel* □ *a historical account of a village in Somerset*.

holey or holy or wholly

These words sound the same, but note the different spellings for the different meanings. Note also that the comparative and superlative forms of ***holey*** and ***holy*** are spelt the same way, **holier** and **holiest**. Also, do not confuse the first two words with **holly**, the plant with red berries.

○ ***holey*** means 'full of holes', as in: *You're not going to wear that holey old cardigan, are you?*

○ ***holy*** means 'sacred', as in: *the Holy Bible*.

○ ***wholly*** means 'entirely, altogether', as in: *I wasn't wholly satisfied with the answer he gave*.

homogeneous or homogenous

Many people confuse these words, especially when pronouncing them, but they are not, in fact, synonymous.

○ When you want to say that something consists or is made up of things 'all of the same kind' in a fairly general way, the word you need is ***homogeneous*** with an *e*, as in: *Even to the extent that they represent a homogeneous group, people with disabilities and learning difficulties represent less than 0.5 per cent of all those enrolled in colleges of further and higher education.*

○ The adjective ***homogenous*** is a synonym for **homologous**, an adjective used only in scientific, specifically biological, contexts and meaning 'having the same structural features' or 'having the same relative position or structure', as in: *In this case, a pair of homologous chromosomes fail to separate from one another during meiosis.*

hopefully

The common use of ***hopefully*** in informal English to mean 'With luck' or 'I hope that' or 'It is hoped that' sends shivers of disapproval down the spines of the many purists who think that this adverb should only be used to mean 'in a hopeful way', as in: *He waited hopefully for the weather to improve*. For this reason, it is best to avoid it in written English, especially in formal or business correspondence.

how

○ Avoid using *how* as a substitute for **that**, eg:

　✗ *Adele told me how she'd had to stand in the rain for an hour.*

　✓ *Adele told me that she'd had to stand in the rain for an hour.*

○ *how* means 'in what way'. It should not be used instead of **why**, eg:

　✗ *'You can't go to the park.' 'How not?'*

　✓ *'You can't go to the park.' 'Why not?'*

however or how ever

Note the different meanings for the one-word and two-word forms.

○ *however* means 'no matter how', or 'in spite of that', as in: *However much we wish for a lottery win, it isn't very likely to happen.* ▫ *He has tried every diet there is. However, he hasn't succeeded in losing much weight.*

○ *how ever* is sometimes used as a more emphatic variant of **how**, as in: *How ever did you manage to lock yourself in the cellar?*

hung or hanged

The usual past tense and past participle of **hang** is *hung*, as in: *The baby chimp hung from a branch by one arm.* ▫ *The paintings were hung in the gallery yesterday and the exhibition starts today.* Note, however, that it is considered incorrect to use *hung* when the verb refers to capital punishment or suicide by hanging. The correct form here is *hanged*, eg:

　✓ *He hanged himself in his prison cell.*

　✗ *He hung himself in his prison cell.*

　✓ *William Wallace was hanged, drawn and quartered.*

　✗ *William Wallace was hung, drawn and quartered.*

hygiene and hygienic

Many people spell these words incorrectly. It's worth learning the spelling by heart.

I

I or me

When is it correct to use *I* and when is it correct to use *me*?

○ Use *I* before a verb when you are the subject of the clause or sentence, as in: *I love old movies.* While few people get this wrong, it is worth noting that *I* is also used before the verb when you are part of the subject; in other words, when other people are included, as in: *Jane and I like gardening.* □ *Jane and Paul and I like gardening.*

○ Use *me* after a verb. Again, this is fairly obvious when *me* stands alone as the object of the clause or sentence, as in: *He gave me a lift home.* However, it is a common error to use *I* instead of *me* when other people are included, eg:

✗ *She gave Alan and I a lift home.*

✓ *She gave Alan and me a lift home.*

✗ *He sends Mum and Dad and I a present every Christmas.*

✓ *He sends Mum and Dad and me a present every Christmas.*

○ Another common error is to use *I* instead of *me* after a preposition, eg:

✗ *Janey sat between Robbie and I.*

✓ *Janey sat between Robbie and me.*

✗ *William waved to Anne and I as he drove away.*

✓ *William waved to Anne and me as he drove away.*

○ Strictly speaking, it is correct to use *I* after the verb *to be*, although very few people use the rather lofty and old-fashioned 'It is I' or 'It was I' these days. 'It's me' or 'It was me' is modern standard usage. However, when there is a following clause, *I* is still used in formal English, as in: *It was I, rather than my partner, who drew up the new will.*

-ible. See **-able**.

-icy or -isy

There are very few words in English that end in **-icy** (*policy, theodicy*) or **-isy** (*hypocrisy, pleurisy*).

➤ See also **-acy** or **-asy**.

-ie- or -ei-

The well-known rule '*i* before *e* except after *c*' can be very useful, provided you are also aware of the many exceptions to the rule. These include: *caffeine, foreign, forfeit, heifer, leisure, protein, seize, sovereign, weir, weird*.

Sometimes, the pronunciation can be used as a further guide to the spelling, in that words with certain pronunciations tend to be spelt either **-ie-** or **-ei-**, as follows:

○ If the vowels are or can be pronounced with an /ay/ sound (as in *may* and *fair*), the spelling is usually **-ei-**, eg: *beige, deign, eight, feign, freight, heir, inveigh, inveigle, neigh, neighbour, reign, rein, sleigh, their, veil, vein, weigh, weight*.

○ If the vowels are or can be pronounced with an /iy/ sound (as in *eye* and *might*), the spelling is usually **-ei-**, eg: *either, Fahrenheit, height, kaleidoscope, neither, seismology, sleight of hand*. But, when the /iy/ sound is followed by *r*, the order of the vowels conforms to the rule '*i* before *e*', eg: *fiery, hierarchy, hieroglyphics*.

○ Following a *c* or a *t* pronounced /sh/, the order is always **-ie-**: *ancient, conscience, deficient, efficient, patience, patient, quotient, species, sufficient*.

ignoramus

The plural is **ignoramuses**.

illegal, illegible and illiterate

Spelling: note the double *l* in all these words.

illusion. See allusion.

imaginary

Note the ending is *-ary* (not *-ery*).

immoral. See amoral.

impassable or impassible

It is important to use the correct spelling for the endings of these words, which have different meanings.

○ **impassable** means 'that cannot be passed or travelled through', as in: *Flood water had made the route impassable*.

○ **impassible** is a formal word meaning 'impassive' or 'incapable of feeling emotion or suffering pain', as in: *The experience of war made him question the metaphysical assumption of an impassible God*.

impel. See **compel**.

impetus

The plural is **impetuses**.

imply or **infer**

It is quite common for people to use **infer** in the sense of **imply**, eg: *Are you inferring that I'm a liar?*

Because **infer** and **imply** have distinct senses, many people regard this use of **infer** as a serious error that displays an inadequate knowledge of English. It is best to be precise and use **imply** and **infer** correctly, even in informal contexts.

○ **imply** means 'to suggest or express (something) indirectly', as in: *What do you mean when you say I need help? Are you implying that I'm not up to the job?* □ *Are you implying that I'm a liar?*

○ **infer** means 'to draw a conclusion from what appears to be suggested or from what one knows', as in: *Am I to infer from what you say that you think I'm not up to the job?* □ *He inferred from her sceptical response that she didn't believe him*.

impracticable or **impractical**

Note the different meanings.

○ **impracticable** means 'not able to be done or used', as in: *With a river on one side and a steep drop on the other, it is impracticable to widen the road*.

○ **impractical** means 'not sensible or efficient or not actually possible', as in: *The plan may have looked good on paper but in reality we found that it was impractical*.

impresario

Notice there is only one *s* in the middle of this word. The plural is **impresarios**.

improvise

Note that the ending is always *-ise* (never *-ize*).

impugn

Pronounced /im-**pyune**/. The *g* is silent.

include. See **comprise**.

incorporate

Notice the spelling with *-por-* (not *-pir-* or *-per-*) in the middle.

incredible or **incredulous**

Do not confuse these words.

○ *incredible* means 'unbelievable', as in: *The whole episode was quite incredible*.

○ *incredulous* means 'showing disbelief, not believing', as in: *'You cannot be serious!' he screamed, his voice incredulous*.

indefinite and **indefinitely**

Spelling: note the *-fin-* and the *-ite* and *-itely* endings.

index

There are two plurals: **indexes** and **indices**. **Indices** is the plural of the mathematical sense 'the number of times a number is multiplied by itself', and is usual for other scientific and technical senses. **Indexes** is the usual plural for lists in books and papers. For other general senses, the plural may be **indexes** or **indices**.

indict and **indictment**

The pronunciation of the *-dict* part of these words rhymes with *bite*, but notice the *c*.

➤ Compare **interdict**.

indifferent and **indifference**

Remember the *-fer-* in the middle, which is often slurred in speech.

infallible

Spelling: notice the double *l*.

infectious or **contagious**

When *infectious* and *contagious* are used to refer to diseases their meanings are different.

○ The germs of *infectious* diseases are carried in and spread through the air.

○ A *contagious* disease is one that can only be spread by direct contact with the sufferer, or with something that they have touched.

But notice there is no real difference in meaning when *infectious* and *contagious* are used figuratively, eg: *infectious laughter* □ *His enthusiasm was contagious.*

infer. See **imply**.

inferior

Notice that when *inferior* is used like a comparative adjective, it must be followed by **to** (not **than**), as in: *Modern chemical dyes are usually considered to be inferior to the natural dyes used in older rugs.*

infinite

Pronunciation: the last syllable should rhyme with *it* (not with *bite*).

infinitive. See **split infinitive**.

inflammable or **flammable**

Spelling: note the double *m*.

These words share the meaning 'capable of catching fire'. *Inflammable* is in general use, but for clarity, and in particular in technical usage, *flammable* is preferred. Note that the opposite is **non-flammable**, (not **non-inflammable**).

inflict. See **afflict**.

ingenious or **ingenuous**

Notice that the spellings of these words differ by only a single letter, though their meanings are quite different.

○ *ingenious* means 'very clever' or 'cleverly made', as in: *That's an ingenious contraption you've built there.*

○ *ingenuous* means 'innocent, open, frank' as in: *On closer examination, the girl had a pleasing appearance, ingenuous but not foolish.*

innocuous

Spelling: notice the double *n*.

innumerable

Notice the double *n*.

inoculate and **inoculation**

Spelling: note the single *n*, single *c* and single *l*.

inseparable

Note the *-par-* in the middle.

insignia

There are two plurals: **insignia** or **insignias**.

instal or install

Both spellings are correct, but *install* is commoner.

instalment or installment

In BrE spelt with single *l*, but in AmE spelt with double *l*.

instil or instill

Spelt with a single *l* in BrE and double *l* in AmE.

intense or intensive

Do not confuse these words, which have different meanings.

○ *intense* means 'very great, extreme', or 'very deep or strong', as in: *intense cold* □ *There's intense competition for places on that course.* □ *an intense blue.*

○ *intensive* means 'concentrated, thorough' or 'taking great care or using much effort', as in: *an intensive training programme* □ *an intensive search.*

interdict

The *-dict* part is pronounced /-dikt/.

➤ Compare **indict**.

interrogate and interrogation

Spelling: notice the double *r*, and the *o*.

interrupt and interruption

Spelling: notice the double *r*.

intrigue

Remember the ending is spelt *-gue*.

invoke. See evoke.

-isy. See -icy.

itinerary

Remember the *-erary* ending, often slurred in speech.

it's or its

Note that adding an apostrophe changes the meaning, so take care to use the correct form in writing.

○ *it's* (with an apostrophe) is the informal short form of 'it is' and 'it has', as in: *It's* [= it is] *nice to meet you.* □ *It's* [= it has] *gone dark all of a sudden.*

○ **its** (without an apostrophe) is the possessive form of **it**, as in:
The moorhen makes its nest in the vegetation close to the water's edge. □ *The car is old and its bodywork is rusting.*

-ize or -ise

For many verbs in BrE, the **-ize** or **-ise** ending is equally accept-able: *organize/organise, publicize/publicise, cauterize/cauterise*.
In AmE, the preferred ending is **-ize**.
There are some words which must be spelt with **-ize**: *capsize, prize* [= to value greatly], *seize*, and *size*.
There are also some words which must be spelt with **-ise**. The commonest are included in the following list:

advise	comprise	exercise	promise
appraise	compromise	franchise	revise
arise	despise	improvise	rise
bruise	devise	incise	supervise
chastise	disguise	liaise	surmise
circumcise	excise	practise	surprise

J

jail. See **gaol**.

jeopardize and **jeopardy**

Remember the *o* in these words. Note that *jeopardize* may be spelt with *-ize* ending.

jeweller or **jeweler**

Spelt with double *l* in BrE, and with single *l* in AmE.

jewellery or **jewelry**

Both words are pronounced /**juul**-ri/. The BrE spelling is *jewellery*, and the AmE spelling *jewelry*.

jodhpurs

Remember the *-d-h-p-* sequence of letters. *Jodhpurs* is a plural noun so takes a plural verb, as in: *Her jodhpurs <u>are</u> muddy.*

join

Many people consider it is faulty style to follow the verb *join* with **together**, because joining by its very nature brings things together. Therefore, it is unnecessary repetition to have both words in the same clause or sentence, eg:

   ✗ *These two young people, who are to be joined together in marriage, …*

   ✓ *These two young people, who are to be joined in marriage, …*

➤ See also **tautology**.

jojoba

Pronounced /hoh-**hoh**-ba/.

➤ Compare **junta**.

judgement or **judgment**

Both spellings are correct, but the one with the *e* tends to be preferred in BrE.

judicial or judicious

Note that these are different words with different meanings.

○ **judicial** means 'of or by judges or law courts', as in: *a judicial review* □ *a fair and reliable judicial system*.

○ **judicious** means 'well judged, prudent', as in: *It was certainly a judicious move to buy up all the surrounding land*.

junction or juncture

Take care not to confuse these words.

○ A **junction** is a place where two things join, as in: *a railway junction* □ *Turn left at the junction of Great George Street and Cranworth Street*.

○ A **juncture** is a particular point in time or in a sequence of events, as in: *At this critical juncture, nothing should be said or done that would jeopardize the negotiations*.

junta

In English, pronounced exactly as it is written.

K

keenness
Notice the double *n*.

kerb. See **curb**.

kibbutz
The plural is **kibbutzim**.

kidnap
In BrE, the *p* is doubled in **kidnapping**, **kidnapped**, and **kidnapper**. In AmE, these may also be spelt **kidnaping**, **kidnaped**, and **kidnaper**.

kind of
In informal English, the structure '**these/those** + *kind of* + plural noun' is commonly used, as in: *These kind of trousers are not fashionable anymore.* □ *Those kind of things are always happening to me.* Despite its frequency, this structure is ungrammatical and should therefore be avoided in formal and written English. Use instead the structure 'plural noun + *of* **this/that** *kind*', or the structure '**this/that** + *kind of* + singular noun', as in: *Trousers of this kind are not fashionable anymore.* □ *That kind of thing is always happening to me.*

knowledge and **knowledgeable**
Notice that the *e* at the end of *knowledge* is not dropped in *knowledgeable*.

L

laboratory
Spelling: note the *o* and the *-atory* ending.

labour and **laborious**
Spelling: notice that the *u* in **labour** is dropped in the adjective **laborious**.

labyrinth
Spelling: note the *y*, which is often slurred in speech.

lacquer
Spelling: notice the *c* followed by *qu*.

ladies. See **gents**.

lama or **llama**
Do not confuse these words.

○ A **lama** is a Tibetan monk.

○ A **llama** is a South American animal.

language
Remember the correct order of the *-ua-* vowel combination when writing this word.

later or **latter**
Take care not to confuse the spellings of these words.

○ **later** is the comparative form of the adjective or adverb **late**.

○ **latter** is an adjective and a noun and refers to the second of two previously mentioned things, or the thing that is towards the end.

lay or **lie**
As verbs, these two words sometimes create difficulties, because of the sense that they share of movement to a flat, horizontal or prone position. Their past tenses and past participles, in particular, are easy to confuse.

○ **lay** means 'to put down carefully or in a flat, horizontal or prone position', as in: *Lay the map out on the grass and hold the corners down with stones.* □ *She carried the sleeping child upstairs and laid him down gently on the bed.* Note that in clauses and sentences where **lay** is the verb, there must be an object, because it is a transitive verb. The past tense and past participle is **laid**.

○ **lie** means 'to be or move into a flat, horizontal or prone position', as in: *He lies on that bed all day staring at the ceiling.* □ *He lay down and tried to get some sleep.* □ *If you hadn't lain in bed all morning, you wouldn't have missed all the fun.* Note that **lie** is an intransitive verb, and therefore does not have an object. The past tense is **lay**, and the past participle is **lain**. Do not use the infinitive **lay** instead of **lie**, eg:

✗ *Surely you're not going to lay in bed all day again?*

In the sense of 'to tell lies', the past tense and past participle of **lie** is **lied**.

lend or loan

Note that **lend** is always a verb, but that **loan** can be a noun or a verb. The use of **loan** as a verb is more common in AmE, but is nonetheless also quite acceptable in BrE, as in: *Will you loan me your bike?* However, it is not standard English to use **lend** as a noun, eg:

✗ *Will you give me a lend of your bike?*

lengthy or long

Both words mean 'of great length', but **lengthy** is usually used to refer to long (and therefore often tedious) speech or writing, as in: *His talk was rather lengthy, and many in the audience were finding it difficult to stay awake.*

leopard

Spelling: remember the *o*, which is not sounded when spoken.

less. See fewer.

liable or likely or apt or prone

These words all have similar but slightly different meanings so care should be taken to use them in the correct context. Note also that **liable to**, **likely to** and **apt to** must be followed by the verb in the infinitive. **Prone to**, on the other hand, can be followed by a noun, a verb in the infinitive, or the *-ing* form of the verb.

○ *liable* means 'runs the risk of, will probably' and usually conveys the idea that there will be unpleasant consequences, especially for the subject of the sentence, and usually this is the result of some previous action or event, as in: *People who play with fire are liable to get burnt.*

○ *likely* means 'will probably' and is correctly used to refer to something happening in a particular set of circumstances, or at a particular place or time, as in: *Since he doesn't drink, he isn't likely to want to go to a pub.* □ *If you don't hurry up, you are likely to miss the beginning of the play.*

○ *apt* and *prone* both mean 'tending to or in the habit of', but *prone* should only be used of people. *Prone* is also preferred when referring to the unpleasant aspects of a person's character or to a tendency for bad or unpleasant things. Compare the following examples: *These tiles are apt to break if you use tile clippers to cut them.* □ *Elderly people are prone to falls, often because of arthritic joints or dizziness.* □ *Nahum was no longer so kind or considerate, and he was prone to strange moods.*

liaise or liaison

These words are frequently misspelled. Take particular care to include the second *i*.

libretto

There are two plurals: **librettos** and **libretti**.

licence and license

In BrE, *licence* is the noun and *license* is the verb. In AmE, *license* is both the noun and the verb.

lie. See lay.

lieutenant

In BrE, the first syllable is pronounced /lef-/. In AmE, it is pronounced /loo-/.

lighted or lit

Lighted and *lit* can both be used as the past tense and past participle of the verb, but *lit* is more usual in BrE, especially for the past tense, eg: *He lit the candles.* In AmE, *lighted* is more usual, eg: *He lighted the candles.*

As an adjective before a noun, *lighted* is more common, as in: *lighted candles.* However, in adjectival phrases, *lit* is commoner, as in: *a dimly lit basement.*

lightening or **lightning**

The spellings of these words are very similar, making them easy to confuse.

○ *lightening* is the present participle of the verb **lighten**, as in: *He smiled, lightening the tension that had grown between them*.

○ *lightning* is a sudden bright flash of electricity in the sky, usually followed by the sound of thunder.

likable or **likeable**

Both spellings are correct.

like or **as**

Notice the following points relating to the use of *like* and *as*.

○ Generally, though not a hard-and-fast rule, *like* is preferred when a real comparison is being made, and *as* when no actual comparison is involved or a comment is being made. *Like* is usually used when what follows is a noun, noun phrase or pronoun, as in: *It feels like silk, but it is a man-made fibre*. □ *Niall sleeps like a hibernating bear*. □ *I don't think he looks like me at all*. In informal English, *like* is sometimes also used before verbs or clauses, but note that for formal contexts *as if* is preferred, eg:

✗ *You look like you need a holiday*.
✓ *You look as if you need a holiday*.

○ Take care to ensure that the comparison being made actually compares the people or things that were intended to be compared. In the first two examples below, 'me' and 'Gordon' are being compared, but the first example wrongly links 'me' and 'dislike'; the third example uses *as* to link 'Gordon's dislike' and 'mine' [= my dislike].

✗ *Like me, Gordon's dislike of any form of confrontation is intense*.
✓ *Like me, Gordon has an intense dislike of any form of confrontation*.
✓ *Gordon's dislike of any form of confrontation is intense, as is mine*.

likely. See **liable**.

lineage

Pronounced /**lin**-i-ij/ and meaning 'ancestry'. Take care to include the *e* in the middle, because **linage** /**line**-ij/ is a different word denoting the number of lines in a printed piece of paper.

liquefy

Notice the *e* before the *-fy*.

liqueur or liquor

Liqueurs are strong sweet alcoholic drinks with various flavours that are usually drunk after a meal. *Liquor* is any alcoholic drink. Remember that *liqueur* is pronounced /li-**kyoor**/ and *liquor* is pronounced /**lik**-or/.

lit. See lighted.

literally

Spelling: notice there is only one *t* in this word.

Careful speakers do not use *literally* unless they mean what they are saying is to be understood in a straightforward literal way, as in: *They'd put super glue on the soles of his boots, so he was literally going nowhere*. The colloquial use of *literally* merely for emphasis is widely regarded as being incorrect, especially when used with an idiomatic expression that is not intended to be understood in a literal way, eg:

✗ *The police have literally gone through the whole place with a fine toothcomb.*

literate and literature

Remember there is only one *t* after the *li-* in these words.

livable or liveable

Both spellings are correct.

llama. See lama.

loan. See lend.

loath or loathe

Take care not to confuse the spellings of these words, which have different meanings.

○ *loath* rhymes with *both*. It means 'unwilling', as in: *I was loath to criticize his work in case I undermined his confidence*. This adjective can also be spelt **loth**.

○ *loathe* rhymes with *clothe*. It is a verb meaning 'to hate or dislike greatly', as in: *They clearly loathed each other*.

long. See lengthy.

longitude

Some people wrongly insert a *t* after the *g* when writing or pronouncing this word.

loose or lose

Do not confuse the spellings of these words.

○ *loose* means 'not tight or not firmly attached', as in: *When the weather is hot, it is more comfortable to wear loose cotton clothing.* □ *Holly's front tooth is loose.*

○ To *lose* means 'to mislay', as in: *This envelope has money in it so be careful not to lose it.*

lot

Avoid using the informal phrases *lots of* or *a lot of* in formal writing. Use instead such expressions as 'a large/great number of', or 'many (of)'.

lovable or loveable

Both spellings are correct, but the form without the *e* is more common.

luggage

Spelling: notice the double *g*.

luxuriant or luxurious

Take care not to confuse these words.

○ *luxuriant* has nothing to do with luxury, but means 'growing strongly or vigorously; abundant, prolific', as in: *The heavy rains have brought luxuriant vegetation to these normally arid islands.* □ *His luxuriant beard was red.*

○ *luxurious* means 'of or relating to luxury or riches', as in: *It is one of the most luxurious health clubs in the country.*

M

machete

Pronounced /ma-**shet**-i/.

magic or magical

Both *magic* and *magical* are used in the sense 'of or relating to magic', but *magical* can also mean 'wonderful, entrancing', as in: *Pack your bags, and prepare yourself for a magical holiday*.

majority. See **bulk**.

manage and manageable

Note that the *e* at the end of *manage* is not dropped in the adjective *manageable*.

manoeuvre and manoeuvrable

These words are often misspelled. Try to memorize the *-oeuvr-* sequence. Notice the *e* at the end of *manouevre* is dropped in the adjective *manoeuvrable*.

manservant

The plural is **menservants** (not **manservants**).

margarine

Spelling: notice the *-gar-* in the middle. Don't be misled by the pronunciation.

masterful or masterly

These words used to be synonymous, but they are now used in different contexts and this distinction is sufficiently useful to be worth maintaining.

- ○ *masterful* means 'showing power or authority', as in: *You're so strong and masterful!*

- ○ *masterly* means 'showing great skill, showing the skill of a master', as in: *this masterly collection of Beethoven symphonies*.

mathematics

This is a singular noun, so takes a singular verb, as in: *Mathematics is not my best subject.*

matter

The phrase '**the fact of the *matter* is**…' has been so overused recently, especially by politicians, that has become a source of irritation to many people, and should where possible be avoided.

➤ See also **cliché**.

may. See can.

me. See I.

media

This word is a plural noun in all its senses. Take care to avoid the error many people make of using a singular verb with *media*, especially when the sense is 'the press', eg:

✗ *The media is camped on his doorstep.*

✗ *The media has been camped on his doorstep for a week.*

✓ *The media are camped on his doorstep.*

✓ *The media have been camped on his doorstep for a week.*

medicine

Note the *i* after the *d*, which is often not sounded when spoken. Note also the *-cine*.

Mediterranean

Note the single *t* and double *r*.

meet or meet with

There is a difference between BrE and AmE usage. In BrE you *meet* a person or people, but *meet with* opposition, approval or misfortune. In AmE, it is correct to use *meet with* for people, as in: *We are going to meet with them on Friday to discuss it.*

memento

There are two spellings of the plural: **mementos** and **mementoes**.

memo

The plural is **memos**.

mendacity or mendicity

Take care not to confuse these words, which, though their spellings are very close to each other, have different meanings.

○ *mendacity* means 'lying', as in: *Politics became synonymous with lawlessness, mendacity and opportunism.*

○ *mendicity* is a formal word meaning 'the state or condition of a beggar'.

meretricious or meritorious

Do not confuse these words.

○ *meretricious* means 'superficially attractive, flashy', as in: *Products range from the truly estimable and inspired to the merely pretty and, sometimes, meretricious.*

○ *meritorious* means 'deserving merit, honour or reward', as in: *A good honours degree or meritorious performance in an ordinary degree is normally required.* □ *awards for gallant or meritorious service.*

messenger

Spelling: note the *-eng-*.

meteorology and meteorological

Notice the second *e* in these words, often slurred in speech.

might. See could.

milage or mileage

Both spellings are correct, though the second is commoner as well as being easier to read.

milennium

Spelling: note the single *l* and the double *n*.

militate or mitigate

Militate is an intransitive verb and is usually used with **for** or **against**. *Mitigate* is a transitive verb and is never used with **against**.

○ *militate* means 'to act upon, have a strong influence or effect on', as in: *the same male attitudes which militate against equality in the home.*

○ *mitigate* means 'to make less severe' or 'to lessen the evil of ', as in: *It would certainly be easier to mitigate the effects of such a drought if long-range forecasting could be made more effective.* □ *I may have been wrong to do it, but that in no way mitigates your own actions.*

The phrase '*mitigate* against' is sometimes wrongly used where what is actually meant is '*militate* against', eg:

✗ *This is certainly a problem which mitigates against the widest acceptance of the language.*

✓ *This is certainly a problem which militates against the widest acceptance of the language.*

millionaire

Spelling: note the double *l* and the single *n*.

miniature

Notice the *a*, which is sometimes not sounded when spoken.

minister and ministry

The *e* in *minister* is dropped in *ministry*.

minuscule

The correct spelling has a *u* after the *n*. It is sometimes written **miniscule**, possibly influenced by its pronunciation and the spelling of the prefix **mini-**. However, this spelling has not yet been accepted as standard and should therefore not be used in writing.

mischievous

Spelling: notice the *-chie-* and the *-vous* ending.
The correct pronunciation is /**mis**-chiv-us/.

mishit

Pronounced /mis-**hit**/ and spelt with a single *s*.

misrelated participle. See dangling participle.

mistletoe

Spelling: notice the *-stle-*. Pronounced /mis-il-**toe**/.

misuse. See abuse.

mitigate. See militate.

mixed metaphor

A metaphor is a figure of speech in which one thing is described in terms of another. The descriptive term applied is figurative rather than literal, as in: *In the Commons today, the Prime Minister came out with all guns blazing.*

A *mixed metaphor* is one in which two or more inconsistent metaphors are combined, as in: *He'll be sailing close to the wind if he doesn't cover his tracks.* This is widely regarded as a stylistic fault, especially when the combined metaphors produce ludicrous or incongruous images, as in: *There are concrete steps in the pipeline.*

mnemonic

Meaning 'something that acts as an aid to memory'. Note the *mne-* is pronounced /nee-/.

moment

The phrase '**at this *moment* in time**' annoys many people, for two reasons: it is a cliché and it is tautological – a moment, by definition, must be in time, and it is considered to be unnecessarily long-winded to have both in the same phrase.

mortgage

Spelling: remember there is a *t* in this word. It comes from the French *mort* (dead) + *gage* (a pledge).

most. See bulk.

motto

There are two spellings of the plural: **mottos** and **mottoes**.

movable or moveable

Both spellings are correct.

mumps

Note that this is a singular noun so takes a singular verb, as in: *With vaccination becoming more widespread, mumps is no longer one of the common childhood illnesses.*

murder and murderous

The *e* is pronounced in ***murder*** but may be slurred in ***murderous***, so take care to include it when writing the adjective.

mutual. See common.

N

naught or nought

In modern English, these words have separate meanings.

○ *naught* means 'nothing', as in: *All his efforts came to naught*.

○ A *nought* is the figure zero (0).

necessary, necessarily and necessity

Remember: single *c* and double *s* in all these words.

need

The verb *need* may be used as an ordinary verb, or as an auxiliary verb (that is, a verb used with other verbs to indicate tense, mood, voice, aspect, etc).

When used as an intransitive verb it inflects like any other ordinary verb: questions and negative statements are formed with the auxiliary verb **do**; and a following verb is preceded by **to**, as in: *If he needs to contact us, he can use his mobile.* □ *You don't need to apologize.* □ *We didn't need to take all this food.* □ *Didn't they need to ask you for help?*

However, as an auxiliary verb, *need* is used only in the present tense, and no *s* is added to the third person singular (he/she/it *need*). Further, as an auxiliary verb, it may be used only in questions where *need* comes before the subject, and in negative statements, as in: *Need we take all this food?* □ *You needn't apologize.*

negation

Take care to avoid errors or ambiguity when a negative word such as **no** or **not** is used in a sentence.

○ If a sentence of two clauses has a negative word such as **not** or **no** which applies to only one of the clauses, take care to structure the sentence so that the negative word does not also include the other clause. Compare the following:

✗ *I don't think the explanation is very clear and needs to be reworded.*

(It is not immediately obvious from this structure whether you do or you don't think it needs to be reworded.)

   ✓ *I think the explanation isn't very clear and needs to be reworded.*

   ✓ *I don't think the explanation is very clear; it needs to be reworded.*

○ When the sentence includes both **not** and **all** or **every**, the sentence should be phrased in such a way that no ambiguity is possible. Consider the following:

   ✗ *All the houses in the street have not got double-glazing.*

(It is not clear whether only some houses have double-glazing, or whether there are no houses with double-glazing.)

Rephrase the sentence in one of the following ways:

   ✓ *Some of the houses in the street have double-glazing.*

   ✓ *Not every house in the street has double-glazing.*

   ✓ *None of the houses in the street have double-glazing.*

➤ See also **double negative**.

neither

Note the following points relating to the usage of *neither*.

○ As a pronoun, *neither* should only be used when referring to one of two people or things, as in: *I asked Bob and Chris, but neither of them knows.* For more than two use **none**, as in: *I asked all the people in the office, but none of them knows.*

○ *Neither* may be followed by a singular or a plural verb in informal English. However, the use of a plural verb is considered by some people to be incorrect, and should be avoided in formal contexts, eg:

   ✗ *Neither of them <u>like</u> beer.*

   ✓ *Neither of them <u>likes</u> beer.*

○ *Neither* should always be paired with *nor* (never with **or**). Both *neither* and *nor* should be placed as close as possible to the word (or words) being contrasted, eg:

   ✓ *The police have found neither a witness nor a suspect.*

   ✗ *The police have neither found a witness nor a suspect.*

○ With *neither*...*nor* comparisons, if the second subject is singular use a singular verb, as in: *Neither the house he lives in nor the car he drives actually <u>belongs</u> to him.* If the second subject is plural, use a plural verb, as in: *Neither Peter nor his sisters <u>know</u> anything about it.*

nine and ninth

Notice the *e* in **nine** is dropped in **ninth**.

none

When used with an uncountable noun **none** takes a singular verb, as in: *None of the furniture was damaged in the move.*

When used with a plural noun **none** can take a singular or plural verb, depending on whether the group as a whole is, or individuals within the group are, being considered, as in: *None of us has ever been abroad.* □ *I've been to a lot of parties, but none were as good as yours.*

notice and noticeable

The *e* at the end of **notice** is not dropped in **noticeable**.

nought. See naught.

nucleus

The plural is **nuclei**.

nuisance

Spelling: note the *-ui-* and the *-ance* ending.

O

O. See **Oh**.

obsolescent or obsolete

Note the slight but important difference in meaning.

- ○ *obsolescent* means 'going out of use' or 'becoming out of date', as in: *Do you think that faxes are obsolescent?*

- ○ *obsolete* means 'no longer in use' or 'already out of date', as in: *He reckons that, by the year 2010, machines like this will be obsolete.*

occasion, occasional and occasionally

These words are all spelt with double *c* and single *s*. Notice also the *-ally* ending in *occasionally* (the *-al-* is often omitted in pronunciation, but the adverb is nonetheless formed from the adjective, not the noun).

occupation and occupy

Notice these words are spelt with double *c* and single *p*.

occur and occurrence

The *r* at the end of *occur* is doubled in the verb forms **occurring** and **occurred**, as well as in the noun *occurrence*. Notice also the ending of the noun is *-ence* (not *-ance*).

-oe- or -e-

Certain words with *-oe-* are now written without the *-o-*, especially in AmE. Note that BrE generally uses the *-oe-* spellings for words such as *amoeba*, *diarrhoea*, *homoeopathic* and *oestrogen*, whereas the preferred AmE spellings are *ameba*, *diarrhea*, *homeopathic* and *estrogen*.

offend and offence or offense and offensive

All these words are spelt with double *f*. The noun is spelt *offence* in BrE, and *offense* in AmE. The adjective *offensive* is spelt with an *s* (never a *c*).

official or **officious**

Note the different meanings.

○ When used as an adjective *official* means 'of or about or done by someone in authority' or 'having authority', as in: *It looks as though the world record has been broken, but we're still waiting for official confirmation of the time.*

○ *officious* means 'adhering too rigidly to rules and regulations' or 'too eager to interfere or offer unwanted advice or assistance', as in: *All those councillors and their officious bureaucrats deserve to be humbled.*

Oh or **O**

○ The *Oh* spelling is the commoner. *Oh* is the form used in modern English. It can be followed by a comma or an exclamation mark: *Oh, what a fright you gave me!* □ *'Oh!' she exclaimed with a look of wide-eyed delight.*

In phrases expressing wishing there may be, or equally correctly may not be, a comma, eg: *Oh for a long cool drink!* □ *Oh, to be at home in my nice warm bed instead of this damp sleeping-bag!*

○ *O* is much rarer, and is usually found only in poetry or religious texts.

older. See **elder**.

omit and **omission**

Both words have single *m*, and *omission* has double *s*. The *t* in **omit** is doubled in the verb forms **omitting** and **omitted**.

one

Note the following points relating to the use of **one**.

○ When *one* is used as personal pronoun, the only pronouns that may be used to refer back to it are **one**, **one's** and **oneself**, eg:

   ✓ *He protested when the police arrested him, saying, 'One must be allowed to protect oneself and one's family!'.*

   ✗ *He protested when the police arrested him, saying, 'One must be allowed to protect himself and his family!'.*

○ When *one* is the subject and a numeral, the verb is singular, as in: *One in three people <u>owns</u> their own home.*

○ When the subject of the verb is a plural noun or noun phrase following *one*, the verb is plural, as in: *He's one of those people who <u>live</u> life to the full.*

one another. See **each other**.

only

The rule that *only* should come immediately before or after the word it emphasizes is rarely followed in informal spoken English, because the speaker's intonation usually makes the meaning clear. However, it is advisable to take more care in formal English, to avoid censure as well as ambiguity. The examples preceded by a tick are more appropriate for formal contexts.

   ✗ *They only speak Gaelic at home.*

   ✓ *They speak only Gaelic at home.*

   ✗ *He only finds time to read when he is on holiday.*

   ✓ *He finds time to read only when he is on holiday.*

opponent

Spelt with double *p* and single *n*.

opportunity and opportunistic

Remember: double *p* in both these words.

opposite and opposition

Spelt with double *p* and single *s*.

optimum

There are two plurals: **optimums** and **optima**.

-or. See -er.

oral. See aural.

ordinance or ordnance

Do not confuse these two words, which have different meanings.

○ An *ordinance* is a law, order or ruling, as in: *The king's ordinances must be obeyed.*

○ *ordnance* is heavy artillery or military supplies.

ordinary

Remember the *a*, which is often slurred in speech.

ours

Remember that *ours* does not have an apostrophe.

outrage and outrageous

Notice that the *e* at the end of *outrage* is retained in the adjective *outrageous*.

overrule

Notice the double *r*, because this word is formed from *over* and *rule*.

owing to. See because of.

P

pajamas. See **pyjamas**.

panel
The final consonant is doubled in the BrE verb forms **panelling** and **panelled**. In AmE, these are usually spelt **paneling** and **paneled**.

panic
Note that a *k* is added in the verb forms **panicking** and **panicked**.

paraffin
Notice the single *r* and double *f*, and the *a* after the *r*.

parallel
Remember: single *r* and double *l*. The final *l* is not doubled in the verb forms **paralleling** and **paralleled**.

paralyse, paralysed and **paralysis**
Remember: single *r*, single *l*, and *y* (not *i*). ***Paralyse*** may also be spelt with *-ze*, but this is more common in AmE.

paraphernalia
Remember the *ph* (pronounced *f*), and the *r* after the *e*.

parcel
The final consonant is doubled in the BrE verb forms **parcelling** and **parcelled**. In AmE, the usual forms are **parceling** and **parceled**.

parliament and **parliamentary**
Remember the *i*, which is often not sounded when spoken. Notice also that the ending of ***parliamentary*** is spelt *-ary*.

partly or **partially**
These words share the broad sense 'not wholly', but note that they are not used synonymously. Take care to use the correct word.

- *partly* means 'in part or in parts' or 'to a certain extent', as in: *The house is built partly in stone and partly in brick.* □ *She's partly responsible for what happened.*

- *partially* means 'not yet to the point of completion' or 'not completely', as in: *The wall is only partially built.*

passed or past

Take care not to confuse the verb form *passed* and the adjective/preposition/adverb/noun *past*.

✗ *I past him in the corridor.*
✓ *I passed him in the corridor.*

passer-by

The plural is **passers-by**.

patrol

The final consonant is doubled in the verb forms **patrolling** and **patrolled**.

peaceable or peaceful

These adjectives are used in slightly different ways.

- *peaceable* usually comes before the noun and is applied to people and their temperaments, or to communities. It means 'peace-loving', 'mild, placid, not inclined to quarrel or fight' or 'existing in peace', as in: *They were a peaceable people.* □ *He's the quiet, peaceable type not normally given to violent outbursts.* □ *Later we reached a walled but obviously peaceable town.*

- *peaceful* can come before or after the noun and is applied to situations, scenes, activities and periods of time. It means 'calm, without disturbance' or 'done in peace', as in: *a peaceful night's sleep* □ *They are striving to achieve a peaceful settlement.* □ *It was quiet and peaceful down by the river.*

pedal

Notice that the final consonant is doubled in the BrE verb forms **pedalling** and **pedalled**. In AmE, the usual forms are **pedaling** and **pedaled**.

pendant or pendent

Both words are nouns and adjectives. Either spelling is correct for both parts of speech, though *pendant* is commoner for the noun, and *pendent* is commoner for the adjective.

peremptory or ~~perfunctory~~

Take care not to confuse these words.

○ *peremptory* means 'that must be complied with', 'allowing no denial or discussion' or 'arrogantly abrupt, imperious', as in: *They have the same force as an order of the court although they are not peremptory.* □ *The voice on the telephone was sharp and peremptory, but I didn't hear too well what it said.*

○ *perfunctory* means 'done merely as a duty or routine, without genuine care or interest', as in: *He gathered his few possessions together and left with only the most perfunctory of farewells.*

perennial

Notice the single *r* and double *n*.

pharaoh

This word often causes spelling problems. Note the *ph* (pronounced *f*) and the *-a-o-h* sequence.

phenomenon

Notice the *ph* (pronounced *f*) and the *-men-*.

The plural is **phenomena**. Take care not to use the plural form *phenomena* as the singular: that is, do not use the plural with a singular verb. This error sometimes leads to the misconception that there is a plural form *phenomenas*.

picnic

Notice that a *k* is added in the verb forms **picnicking** and **picnicked**.

piteous or pitiable or pitiful

Pitiful and *pitiable* may be used synonymously in the senses 'very sad, arousing or deserving pity', as in: *The old man was in a pitiable/pitiful condition.* They also share the sense 'very bad, very poor, arousing or deserving contempt', as in: *That was a pitiful attempt at a smile!* □ *That was a pitiable attempt you made.* The only important difference between *pitiful* and *pitiable* is that *pitiful* is more likely to be used to describe an inanimate object.

Piteous also means 'arousing or deserving pity', as in: *The sobs were uncontrollable and she gave a long piteous cry.* Notice, however, that *piteous* cannot be used in the sense 'arousing or deserving contempt', eg:

✗ *That was a piteous attempt at a smile!*

plead

The usual BrE past tense and past participle is **pleaded**. However, in AmE and some regional variants of BrE, particularly Scottish English, **pled** is also used for the past tense.

plus

Plus is sometimes used in informal English to mean 'and also', as in: *They've just heard that they've won their court case, plus they had that lottery win recently, so they're over the moon*.

This use of *plus* is not appropriate for formal speech or writing.

pore or pour

Don't confuse the spelling of these words.

○ As a verb, *pore* means 'to study closely', as in: *He pored over the account books, trying to find the error amongst the endless columns of figures*. As a noun, *pore* denotes a small opening in skin or on the surface of a plant.

○ To *pour* means 'to allow liquid to flow from a container', as in: *Shall I pour you a nice cup of tea?*

portentious or pretentious

These words are synonymous when applied to people and the way they express themselves, sharing the sense 'grandiose, self-important', as in: *He had adopted a portentous/pretentious tone suitable for expressing admiration for the Greatest Living Englishman*. **Pretentious** is used more broadly to refer to anything that is grandiose, showy or affected, and is the commoner of the two words.

Note that *portentious* also means 'ominous, fateful', as in: *The split reflected a portentous difference of approach within the Party*. In this sense it is not a synonym of *pretentious*.

Portuguese

Spelling: remember the *u* after the *g*.

posthumous

Pronounced /**pawst**-you-mus/. Don't forget the *h* when writing this word.

pour. See pore.

practicable or practical

There is a slight but important difference in the meanings of these words.

- **practicable** means 'able to be carried out or used', as in: *We must come up with a plan that is both practicable and cost-efficient.*
- **practical** means 'sensible or efficient' or 'actually possible', as in: *a practical solution.*

Thus, two different courses of action may be **practicable**, but one may be more **practical** than the other. Note also that **practical** can be applied to people, but **practicable** is only applied to things, ideas, plans, suggestions, etc.

practice or practise

In BrE, the form with the *c* is the noun and the form with the *s* is the verb. In AmE **practise** is used for both the noun and the verb.

pray or prey

These words are pronounced in the same way, so take care to use the correct spelling in writing.

- To **pray** is 'to give thanks to or ask one's god for something'.
- An animal's **prey** is the creatures it hunts, kills and eats.

precede

Note the *-cede* ending.

➤ See also **proceed**.

precipitate or precipitous

The adjective **precipitous** is sometimes used in the sense of 'hasty'. This is widely regarded as being incorrect, and it is best to maintain the distinction between the two words.

- **precipitate** means 'reckless, hasty or ill-considered', as in: *It would not be wise to make precipitate and unilateral cuts to our armed forces.*
- **precipitous** means 'very steep, like a precipice', as in: *a precipitous route* □ *The site is suitably romantic, on its precipitous hillside above the small village of Midford.*

predecessor

Spelling: single *c*, double *s*, and *-or* ending.

prefer and preferable and preference

Note that the *r* at the end of **prefer** is not doubled in the adjective **preferable** or the noun **preference**. However, the *r* is doubled in the verb forms **preferring** and **preferred**.

○ Both *prefer* and *preferable* should be followed by **to** (not **than**), eg:

✓ *I prefer coffee to tea.*

✗ *I prefer coffee than tea.*

✓ *Death would be preferable to the suffering she has had to endure.*

✗ *Death would be preferable than the suffering she has had to endure.*

○ *preferable* should not be preceded by **more** or **most**.

prescribe or proscribe and prescriptive or proscriptive

The verbs *prescribe* and *proscribe*, and the adjectives *prescriptive* and *proscriptive*, are sometimes confused. This is a serious error because use of the wrong word may give the opposite meaning to that which is intended.

○ To *prescribe* means 'to recommend or order officially' and 'to lay down or establish (a duty, penalty, rule, etc)', as in: *It gives the Secretary of State the power to prescribe which books should be studied in the classroom. □ You must not prescribe aims and preferences for art.*

○ To *proscribe* means 'to forbid, outlaw or ban', as in: *The predictions of economic theory are not sufficiently clear-cut to permit us to proscribe monopoly outright. □ This book was formerly proscribed by the church.*

presume or assume

These words are sometimes used synonymously, but there is a distinction between them which is valuable enough to be maintained.

○ To *presume* means 'to suppose (something to be the case) based on the facts available', as in: *We had heard nothing for months, so presumed he was dead.*

○ To *assume* means 'to accept something is so, to take for granted', as in: *If we assume that he's dead, we'll have to do something to provide for his family.*

pretentious. See portentious.

prevaricate or procrastinate

Take care not to confuse these words.

○ To *prevaricate* means 'to talk in an evasive way, in order to avoid a direct or truthful answer, coming to the point, etc', as in: *When he asked what I was going to do I knew that I would have to prevaricate or face problems.*

○ To **procrastinate** means 'to put off to some later time something that ought to be dealt with now', as in: *Don't procrastinate; make a start on each project as soon as possible.*

prey. See **pray**.

principal or **principle**

Don't confuse the spellings of these words, which have different meanings.

○ *principal* is an adjective as well as a noun. It means 'main or most important', as in: *He gave as the principal reason for his resignation lack of cooperation from colleagues.*

○ *principle* is a noun meaning 'rule' or 'theory', as in: *the principles of English grammar* □ *I'm not going to sacrifice my principles for money.*

prisoner

Don't forget the *o*, which is often slurred in speech.

privilege and **privileged**

These words have no *d* before the *g*.

proceed

Note the *-ceed* ending.

Do not confuse **proceed** meaning 'to go on or forward' with **precede** meaning 'to go before'.

procrastinate. See **prevaricate**.

profession and **professional**

Spelling: single *f* and double *s*.

program or **programme**

In AmE all senses are spelt **program**. In BrE all senses, except the computer-related sense, are spelt **programme**.

prone. See **liable**.

pronounce and **pronunciation**

Notice that **pronounce** has *-ou-* after the first *n*, but the noun **pronunciation** drops the *o* after the first *n*, and is said as it is spelt.

proscribe and **proscriptive**. See **prescribe**.

prove and **provable**

Note that the *e* at the end of *prove* is dropped in the adjective *provable*.

public and **publicly**

Notice that *-ly* (not *-ally*) is added to *public* to form the adverb *publicly*.

purposefully or **purposely**

These words are sometimes confused.

○ *purposefully* means 'with purpose' and refers to a person's manner or determination, as in: *He strode purposefully into his boss's office, clearly determined to settle the question of his long-overdue promotion.*

○ *purposely* means 'intentionally, on purpose', as in: *They purposely misled us.*

pyjamas or **pajamas**

The first spelling is used in BrE, the second is used only in AmE.

pyramid

Notice the *y*.

Q

questionnaire

Spelling: notice the double *n*, and the *e* at the end.

The first syllable may be pronounced /kwest-/ or, less commonly, /kest-/.

quiet and quite

When writing these words take care to use the correct spellings, which are sometimes confused.

➤ See also **quite** below.

quit

Note the *t* is doubled in the verb forms **quitting** and **quitted**. The AmE past tense and past participle **quit** is also now common in BrE, as in: *She quit her job.* ◻ *She's quit.*

quite

Take care when you are using *quite* in written English. Notice that in such constructions as, 'I'm quite warm now', the meaning can be 'I'm completely warm now' or 'I'm fairly warm now'. While this is unlikely to be misinterpreted in spoken English, where the intonation and context usually helps to make clear what is meant, it is probably better to rephrase the sentence in written English to avoid any ambiguity.

R

ratable or rateable
Both spellings are correct, but the form with the *e* is easier to read.

raze
Some people think the expression 'to *raze* to the ground' is tautological, since *raze* means 'to demolish completely'.

really
Remember the *-ly* ending is added to *real*, doubling the *l*.

reason
The tradition rule was that *reason* should only be followed by **that**, and not by **why** or **because**. However, **why** and **because** are so common in everyday speech there is no real justification for continuing to adhere to this rule, except in formal contexts.

✓ *The reason he objected was <u>that</u> he felt he was not being treated fairly.* [= formal usage]
✓ *The reason <u>why</u> he objected was that he felt he was not being treated fairly.*
✓ *The reason <u>why</u> he objected was because he felt he was not being treated fairly.*

rebel, rebellion, and rebellious
Notice that the final *l* in *rebel* is doubled in *rebellion* and *rebellious*, and also in the verb forms **rebelling** and **rebelled**.

recede
Note this is spelt *-cede* (not *-sede*).

receipt
This word is frequently misspelled, even though it conforms to the rule '*i* before *e* except after *c*'. Notice the *p* before the *t*.

recognize or recognise
Both spellings are correct in BrE. Remember to include the *g*, which is sometimes slurred in speech.

recommend and recommendation

These words are often misspelled. Remember: single *c* and double *m*.

reconnaissance

Another word that is difficult to spell. Note the single *c*, then double *n*, then double *s*.

reconnoitre or reconnoiter

The *-re* ending is used in BrE, and the *-er* ending in AmE. Note the double *n* and the *-o-i-t-* sequence of letters.

recur, recurrence and recurrent

The final *r* of *recur* is doubled in *recurrence* and *recurrent*, and also in the verb forms **recurring** and **recurred**. Notice also the *-ence* (not *-ance*) and *-ent* (not *-ant*) endings.

redundant and redundancy

The endings are *-ant* (not *-ent*) and *-ancy* (not *-ency*).

refer and referral

The final consonant of *refer* is doubled in *referral* and in the verb forms **referring** and **referred**.

referable or referrable

Both spellings are correct.

refrigerator

Spelling: don't include the *d* from *fridge* in *refrigerator*.

refute or deny

These words are not synonymous, despite the common use of *refute* in the sense '*deny* emphatically', eg: *The minister refutes any suggestion of wrongdoing.*

○ To *refute* means 'to prove or show to be false', as in: *The documentary evidence will refute any suggestion of wrongdoing on the part of the minister.*

○ To *deny* means 'to declare not to be true', as in: *The minister denies that there has been any wrongdoing.* □ '*Do you deny that you were at the scene?*'

remittance or remission

Do not confuse these words, which are both derivatives of **remit**.

○ *remittance* is a term used in business correspondence for money that is sent in payment for something, as in: *Thank you for your remittance in settlement of our July invoice.*

○ *remission* denotes the lessening of something, such as a prison sentence or the effects of a chronic or malignant disease, as in: *The reason for the remissions experienced by certain patients is not fully understood.*

restaurant

Take care with the spelling of this word, whose second syllable is often slurred in speech.

review or revue

Don't confuse the spellings of these words, which have different senses.

○ A *review* is a report, study or critical assessment of something.

○ A *revue* is a type of humorous, often satirical, theatre show that includes songs, sketches, etc.

rheumatism

Spelling: remember the *rheu-* sequence.

rhododendron

Spelling: notice the *rh* and the second *o*.
There are two plurals: **rhododendrons** and **rhododendra**.

rhyme and rhythm

Remember these words have *h* then *y* after the *r*.

ridiculous

A frequently misspelled word, probably because it is often pronounced as if it began with *re-*.

righteous

Notice the *e* before the *-ous*.

rigour or rigor and rigorous

For the noun, the form with the *u* is used in BrE, and the form without is used in AmE. The adjective *rigorous* is spelt the same way in both BrE and AmE.

rostrum

There are two plurals: **rostrums** and (more rarely) **rostra**.

S

sacrilege and sacrilegious

Despite the usual association these words have with **religion**, which may lead you to think that they are spelt in the same way, they are spelt with *-ril-* (not *-rel-*).

sailer or sailor

Do not confuse these two words, which have different meanings.

○ *sailer* is used of sailing boats and ships, as in: *This boat is built for cruising rather than racing and so isn't a very fast sailer.*

○ *sailor* is used of people, as in: *She's married to a sailor.* □ *He's not a good sailor. He gets very seasick.*

salable or saleable

Both spellings are correct but the second one is more common, probably because it is easier to read.

satiable

Pronounced /**say**-sha-bl/, but note the ending is spelt *-iable*.

scales

This is a plural noun so always takes a plural verb, as in: *These scales <u>are</u> not very accurate.*

scarcely. See **barely**.

scarf

There are two plurals: **scarfs** or **scarves**.

sceptic or skeptic

The first spelling is used in BrE, the second in AmE.

schedule

Notice the *sch-* spelling.

In BrE, pronounced /**shed**-jool/, and in AmE /**sked**-yool/. The AmE pronunciation is being used increasingly in BrE.

scissors

This is a plural noun so always takes a plural verb, as in: *The kitchen scissors are in that drawer*.

Scotch, **Scottish**, and **Scots**

Care should be taken in the use of these words to avoid giving offence or causing irritation to the people of Scotland.

○ **Scotch** is now only used when referring to the whisky produced in Scotland, or in the names of certain foods, such as *Scotch broth* and *Scotch eggs*. Do not use this word when referring to a person from, or the language of, Scotland.

○ **Scottish** is the word most used when referring to people or things from Scotland, as in: *Scottish beef* □ *a Scottish accent* □ *the Scottish Borders* □ *His parents are Scottish* □ *You're Scottish, aren't you?*

○ **Scots** is usually used to refer to the dialect of English spoken in Scotland, as in: *a Scots dictionary* □ *a Scots accent*. You can also refer to a person from Scotland as a *Scot*, as in: *He was proud to be a Scot*.

➤ See also **English**.

scurrilous

Spelling: note the double *r*, single *l* and *-ous* ending.

-se. See **-e**.

secateurs

Note the *-eurs* spelling. This is a plural noun so always takes a plural verb, as in: *The secateurs have been sharpened*.

-sede. See **-cede**.

seek

The past tense and the past participle is **sought**, as in: *He sought to pacify the angry demonstrators*.

sensual or **sensuous**

Note the different meanings.

○ **sensual** means 'of or concerning the physical senses'. *Sensual* is usually applied to pleasurable feelings experienced by the body rather than the mind, especially sexual arousal, as in: *a sensual mouth* □ *Even the way she turned her head, in that slow deliberate fashion, was sensual*.

○ **sensuous** means 'affecting or perceived through the senses, especially in a pleasant way'. The pleasure is usually of the mind rather than the body, and therefore music or art can be *sensuous*.

separate and separable

These words are frequently misspelled. Notice the -*par*- (not -*per*-). Also note that *separable* ends -*able* (not -*ible*).

sergeant

Remember this word is spelt -*geant*. The variant spelling **serjeant** is much rarer, and is used only in the titles of certain officials.

Shakespearean or Shakespearian

Both spellings are correct, but the first is more common.

shall or will

For formal standard speech or writing the basic rules regarding the use of **shall** and **will** are as follows:

○ With the simple future tense, and with offers or suggestions, use **shall** with the first person and **will** with the second and third person, as in: *I shall be arriving tomorrow morning.* □ *You will be in Paris by six o'clock.* □ *Shall we go home tomorrow?*

○ When talking about the future, and at the same time expressing permission, determination, compulsion, etc, use **will** with the first person and **shall** with the second and third person, as in: *I will not do it!* □ *You shall help to tidy up, whether you like it or not!* □ *We will be there, don't worry.*

shampoo

The plural and the third person present singular is **shampoos**. The present participle is **shampooing**, and the past tense/past participle is **shampooed**.

sheik or sheikh

Both spellings are correct.

sheath or sheathe

The form without the *e* is the noun, and the form with the *e* is the verb. Notice that when -*ing* and -*ed* are added to the verb this last *e* is dropped.

shed

The past tense and past participle of the verb is **shed** (not *shedded*), as in: *The trees had shed their leaves.*

shrink

The past tense of the verb is **shrank** and the past participle is **shrunk** (changed to **shrunken** when used as an adjective).

shyer or shier and shyest or shiest

The comparative and superlative forms of the adjective **shy** can be spelt with a *y* or *i*.

similar or analogous

Remember that these words are not true synonyms, since ***analogous*** means '*similar* in some respects only'.

sink

The past tense of the verb is **sank** and the past participle is **sunk** (changed to **sunken** when used as an adjective).

sizable or sizeable

Both spellings are correct.

ski

Because this word ends in *i*, many people are unsure of the spellings of the plural and verb forms. The plural and the third person singular are spelt **skis**. The present participle is **skiing**. The past tense and past participle may be spelt **skied** or **ski'd**.

skilful or skillful

The first spelling is used in BrE, and the second only in AmE.

slyer or slier and slyest or sliest

The comparative and superlative forms of the adjective **sly** can be spelt with a *y* or *i*.

smooth

The spelling of the adjective and the verb are the same. It is not correct to add an *e* to the end of the verb.

somersault

Notice the *o* and the *-au-*.

soprano

The plural is **sopranos**.

speciality or specialty

The commonest meaning of these words is the same, as in: *Fish dishes are our chef's speciality/specialty*. The main difference is that ***speciality*** is more common in BrE, and ***specialty*** is more common in AmE.

specially or especially

Because they share the notion of something that is special, these words are sometimes confused.

○ *specially* means 'for a special purpose' or 'solely for', as in: *She has driven up from London specially to meet my parents.* □ *I made this cherry cake specially for you.*

○ *especially* means 'particularly' or 'above all', as in: *She was especially late that day.* □ *I like drawing and painting, especially portraits.*

Do not use *especially* when you should use *specially*, eg:

✗ *She has driven up from London especially to meet my parents.*

species

The plural is **species**.

spectrum

There are two plurals: **spectra** and **spectrums**.

spin

This verb has the past tense and the past participle **spun**. Notice the doubling of the *n* in the present participle **spinning**.

split

This verb has the past tense and the past participle **split**. Notice the doubling of the *t* in the present participle **splitting**.

split infinitive

In English, the infinitive is made up of the word 'to' and the base form of the verb, eg: *to see*. Thus, an infinitive is split when a word, usually an adverb, is inserted between the 'to' and the verb, as in: *He wanted to quickly clear up any misunderstanding.* □ *They expect us to meekly accept every increase, no matter how great.*

Some traditionalists claim that this is ungrammatical and should always be avoided. However, in modern English grammars, the tendency is to differentiate between rules which ought to be adhered to, and style guidance which is generally less rigid and prescriptive. Modern grammars make the point that the 'rule' on splitting infinitives was borrowed in the nineteenth century from Latin grammar where a split infinitive is not possible (there is no 'to' + verb structure in Latin), and that its application to English is therefore illogical and unjustified.

The modern consensus then is that it is not strictly ungrammatical to insert an adverb between 'to' and the verb, and that it should only be avoided where it would produce an inelegant construction: that is, for stylistic reasons. If you feel you must avoid a split infinitive, it is usually possible to rephrase the sentence, or to change the verb so that the adverb is superfluous. Be aware, however, that the simple expedient of moving the adverb can alter the emphasis, the rhythm, or even the sense, and the result may not be entirely satisfactory. Compare the sentences below, the first of which is probably the most famous example of a split infinitive:

To boldly go, where no man has been before.

To go boldly, where no man has been before.

Boldly to go, where no man has been before.

Ignoring the element of familiarity which in itself makes the original version acceptable to most people even if they are aware that an infinitive has been split, notice that shifting the adverb changes the emphasis and so the rhythm of the whole sentence.

There are a couple of specific points to be kept in mind. These are:

○ Some modifying words like **only** and **really** must come between 'to' and the verb in order to convey the correct meaning, as in: *I want you to really think about this.*

○ There are certain constructions in which it is stylistically preferable not to split an infinitive. For example, with negative words like **not** or **never**, as in:

✗ *Be careful to not step on the wet concrete.*

✓ *Be careful not to step on the wet concrete.*

✗ *He vows to never go to another Wagner opera.*

✓ *He vows never to go to another Wagner opera.*

squalor

Note that there is no *u* after the *o*.

stadium

There are two plurals: **stadiums** (in general use) and **stadia**. Both are quite correct, though many traditionalists prefer the *-a* ending (borrowed from Latin), and modernists prefer the regular plural formed by adding an *s*.

stalactite and stalagmite

The spellings are a clue to which grow down from the ceiling and which grow up from the floor; *-c-* for ceiling and *-g-* for ground.

start. See **begin**.

stationary or **stationery**

It is a very common error to get the spellings of these words confused.

○ **stationary** is an adjective meaning 'not moving'.

○ **stationery** is a noun meaning 'writing materials'

still life

The plural is **still lifes**.

stink

There are two past tenses of this verb: **stank** or **stunk**. The past participle is **stunk**.

strive

The past tense is **strove** and the past participle is **striven**.

stupefy

Notice the *-e-* before the *-fy*.

subtle and **subtly**

Notice the *b* in these words, and that the *e* in **subtle** is dropped in the adjective **subtly**.

succeed, **success** and **successor**

All these words are spelt with double *c*. Notice too that while **succeed** has double *e*, **success** and **successor** have only one *e* and double *s*.

suddenness

Notice the double *d* and, in particular, the double *n*.

suitable

Remember: the ending is *-able* (not *-ible*).

supervise

The ending is always *-ise* (never *-ize*).

supplely

Notice the *e* is retained in this word, though it is not sounded when spoken.

susceptible

Notice the *-sc-* and the *-ible* ending.

swap or **swop**

Both spellings are correct. The *p* is doubled in the verb forms **swapping/swopping** and **swapped/swopped**.

swat or swot

Remember that the different spellings *swat* and *swot* have different meanings, unlike **swap** and **swop** above. The final consonant is doubled in the verb forms **swatting/swotting** and **swatted/swotted**.

○ *swat* means 'to hit with a heavy slapping blow', as in: *He swatted the fly with a rolled-up newspaper.*

○ *swot* is an informal word meaning 'to study hard', as in: *She's been swotting for her GCSEs.*

swell

The past tense is **swelled** and the past participle is **swollen** or **swelled**.

syllabus

There are two plurals: **syllabuses** or (less commonly) **syllabi**.

synopsis

The plural is **synopses**.

T

taboo or tabu
Both spellings are correct, though the first is more common.

tamable or tameable
Both spellings are correct.

tautology
Tautology is a fault in style in which a word (or a group of words) is added, repeating the meaning of a word (or words) already used in the phrase or sentence. Unnecessary repetition of this kind may invite censure, or even ridicule, and should be avoided where possible. Some of the commonest and most obvious examples of tautology are included in the following sentences, with the superfluous word in brackets: *We progressed (forward) slowly.* ▫ *We continued (on) for several miles.* ▫ *The Dutch players are retreating (back) to their (own) half.* ▫ *It sank (down) to the bottom.* ▫ *Please refer to the tables enclosed (herewith).* ▫ *the (past) history of his family* ▫ *their (mutual) respect for each other* ▫ *their mutual respect (for each other)* ▫ *I (myself personally) am not involved in the dispute.*

taxi
The plural can be spelt **taxis** or **taxies**. The verbs forms are: third person present singular **taxis** or **taxies**; present participle **taxiing** or **taxying**; past tense and past participle **taxied**.

-tch. See -ch.

teachable
The ending is spelt *-able* (not *-ible*).

tempo
There are two plurals: **tempos** and **tempi**.

terminus
There are two plurals: **terminuses** and **termini**.

testes

The singular is **testis**.

than

In formal English, when ***than*** in a comparison is followed by a personal pronoun, all pronouns (except *who*) must be in the subjective case (i.e. *I, he, she, we, they*), as in: *There is no finer draughtsman than he.* However, in informal speech and writing, it is common and quite acceptable to use the objective case (i.e. *me, him, her, us, them*).

➤ See also **what**.

that

It is quite acceptable, even in formal contexts, to use the relative pronoun ***that*** in constructions such as *'The man that I met happened to be Ken's uncle.'* It is not necessary to replace ***that*** with '**who**', '**whom**' or '**which**', as some people think.

their, **there** or **they're**

Take care to use the correct spelling.

○ ***their*** means 'belonging to them', as in: *They can do what they like in their own home.*

○ ***there*** means 'at, in, or to that place', as in: *There they can do as they please; it is their retreat from the world.*

○ ***they're*** is the short form of 'they are', as in: *They're moving their desks over there.*

theirs and **there's**

Remember that ***theirs*** [= belonging to them] does not have an apostrophe, and ***there's*** (the short form of 'there is') has an apostrophe.

there. See **here**.

thesaurus

There are two plurals: **thesauruses** and **thesauri**.

thesis

The plural is **theses**.

thrive

Note that the past tense is **throve** or **thrived**, and the past participle is **thriven** or **thrived**.

tic or **tick**

Note that the form without the *k* denotes a habitual nervous involuntary movement of a muscle, especially in the face. All other senses are spelt with a k.

-tion or -sion or -cion

Words with these endings are frequently misspelled.

Note there are only two common words that end in *-cion*: *coercion* and *suspicion*.

For the *-tion* and *-sion* endings, there are no hard-and-fast rules that help to decide which ending is correct. It is therefore more straightforward to list the commonest words for each ending so that their spellings can be checked.

Below is a list of common words ending in *-tion*

abstention	contravention	fiction	position
abortion	deception	infection	prevention
action	digestion	intention	proportion
addition	disruption	intervention	ration
adoption	distortion	meditation	retention
assertion	education	mention	rotation
attention	exemption	nation	solution
caption	exertion	notion	station
combustion	exhaustion	option	suggestion
contention	extortion	portion	taxation

Below is a list of common words ending in *-sion*

accession	decision	extension	procession
adhesion	dimension	immersion	propulsion
admission	division	incision	recursion
ascension	fusion	mansion	scansion
aspersion	emulsion	pension	submersion
comprehension	expansion	permission	vision
confusion	expulsion	persuasion	version

➤ See also **-ction**.

titillate or titivate

Do not confuse these words, which have different meanings.

○ **titillate** means 'to excite, especially in a sexual way', as in: *lurid sensationalism designed to titillate local audiences.*

○ **titivate** means 'to smarten up by making small improvements, to put the finishing touches to', as in: *'Go and titivate yourself if you must, and be down in the bar in ten minutes.'*

tonsillitis

Notice the double l.

too. See **also**.

tortuous or **torturous**

The spellings of these words are almost the same, but they have different meanings.

○ *tortuous* means 'full of twists and turns', as in: *a tortuous route over the mountains*.

○ *torturous* means 'like or involving torture', as in: *Then there was a torturous wait for the results of the biopsy*.

toward or **towards**

In their general sense, there is no difference in meaning. *Towards* is commoner in BrE and *toward* is commoner in AmE.

traffic

Notice a *k* is added in the verb forms **trafficking** and **trafficked**.

tranquilize or **tranquillise** or **tranquillize**

The form with the single *l* and *-ize* is used in AmE. The form with the double *l* and *-ise* or *-ize* is used in BrE.

transfer

Note that the *r* is doubled in the verb forms **transferring** and **transferred**.

transferable or **transferrable**

Both spellings are correct, though the first is more common.

transpire

Transpire is sometimes used loosely in informal English as a synonym for 'to happen', rather than 'to come to light', eg:

✗ *What transpired after you told him he was sacked?*

✓ *It transpired that some people were more susceptible to the poison than others.*

troop or **troupe**

The first spelling is used for a group of soldiers. The second is used either for a group of entertainers, or for a group of monkeys.

try

In formal speech and writing, use *try to* rather than *try and*, eg:

✓ *Try to remember what he looked like.*

✗ *Try and remember what he looked like.*

twelfth

Remember: *f* before the *th*.

U

uninterested or disinterested

Notice the difference in meaning.

○ *uninterested* means 'not interested, not taking an interest', as in: *She seemed quite uninterested in anything I had to say.* ❑ *He's uninterested in sport.*

○ *disinterested* means 'impartial, unbiased', as in: *What we need is a disinterested third party who can judge the issue fairly.* *Disinterested* is sometimes used when *uninterested* is meant, eg:

✗ *He seems disinterested in sports or team games.*

unique

By definition, if something is *unique* there is only one of it, or it has no equal. *Unique* does not mean 'unusual', 'remarkable' or 'rare', and it is therefore incorrect to modify it with adverbs such as 'fairly', 'pretty' and 'rather', eg:

✗ *It was a fairly unique experience.*
✗ *His was rather a unique talent.*

unshakable or unshakeable

Both spellings are correct.

unsocial or unsociable or antisocial

When these words are applied to a person, they all mean 'disliking or avoiding the company of other people'. However, *unsocial* is also applied to working hours (in the evening or during the night), which prevent a person from taking part in normal social activities. *Antisocial* is also applied to behaviour and means 'harmful or upsetting to other people'.

urban or urbane

Urban means 'of or concerning a town or city', but *urbane* means 'sophisticated, elegant'. Take care not to confuse their spellings.

us. See **we**.

usable or **useable**

Both spellings are correct.

usual and **usually**

These words are sometimes spelt or typed incorrectly. Remember the second *u* followed by *a*, and the double *l* in ***usually***.

V

vaccinate and **vaccination**
Spelling: note the double c and single n.

vacuum
Remember: single c and double u.

value and **valuable**
Notice that the e at the end of *value* is dropped in the adjective *valuable*.

vegetable
Remember the second e between the g and the t.

vehement and **vehemence**
Do not forget the -he- when writing either of these words.

vehicle
Notice the h, which is not pronounced in *vehicle*, but is pronounced in the related adjective **vehicular**.

venal or **venial**
These words have different meanings and should not be confused.

○ *venal* means 'able to be bribed' or 'associated with bribery', as in: *However corrupt and venal a politician he might have been before, once elected president it is assumed that he changes.*

○ *venial* means 'forgivable', as in: *The list of sins, venial and otherwise, was long.*

video
The plural is **videos**.

vigour and **vigorous**
Notice that the u in *vigour* is dropped in the adjective *vigorous*.

voluntary
Spelling: remember the a before the -ry.

W

waive or wave

These words are pronounced in the same way, but note that they are not variant spellings of the same word. The form with the *i* means 'to refrain from insisting on (a rule, claim, right, etc)'.

want or wont

Do not use *want* when you should use *wont*. As an adjective, *wont* means 'accustomed, habitually inclined' as in: *He was wont to rise early*. As a noun, it denotes a habit that someone has, as in: *It was her wont to rise early and open all the windows*.

we or us

It is a common error to use *we* instead of *us* when 'I and others' is the part of the object of a verb, eg:

✗ *This is the busiest time of the year for we farmers.*

✓ *This is the busiest time of the year for us farmers.*

The easiest way to check which is correct is to leave out 'farmers' in the above example and it becomes clear that the correct form is 'for us'.

weave

When the sense is 'to wind in and out' and 'to move to and fro', **weaved** is the past tense and the past participle, as in: *She weaved towards the door, finding her vision blurring, her legs beginning to go weak.*

For the sense 'to make cloth', the past tense is **wove** and the past participle is **woven**.

were

In formal writing, *were* should be used instead of **was** in conditional sentences, as in: *If I were a rich man I wouldn't have to work hard.* ◻ *If it weren't so cold, we could go for a walk.* ◻ *Were he to resign now, he would forfeit a proportion of his pension.*

what

Note the following points relating to the use of **what**.

○ In the sentence '*What we need is colouring pencils and paper*', notice that the verb is singular. Some people make the mistake of thinking that because there is a plural noun following the verb, the verb should also be plural, eg:

✗ *What we need are colouring pencils and paper.*

✓ *What we need is colouring pencils and paper.*

○ **What** can only follow **than** in comparisons when it means 'that which' or 'the thing(s) which', as in: *Those are cheaper than what they had on offer last week.*

Otherwise, it is not acceptable in standard English to use **what** after **than** in comparisons, eg:

✗ *She can do it better than what I can.*

✓ *She can do it better than I can.*

○ It is not acceptable in standard English to use **what** after nouns and pronouns, eg:

✗ *It was the shock what killed him.*

✓ *It was the shock that killed him.*

what or which

Both **what** and **which** may be used when asking questions about a choice. **What** is usually used when the choice is unlimited or unspecified: *What is the quickest way to get rid of those extra pounds?* **Which** is usually used when the choice is from a known or limited number of options, as in: *Which is the best diet?*

whatever or what ever

Note the different meanings for the one-word and two-word forms.

○ **whatever** means 'no matter what', as in: *Whatever I say, he always disagrees with me.*

○ **what ever** is sometimes used as a more emphatic variant of '**what**', as in: *What ever are you doing in that ditch?*

whereabouts

As a noun, **whereabouts** can take a singular or plural verb, as in: *His present whereabouts is/are unknown.*

whereby

The correct meaning of **whereby** is 'by means of which' or 'according to which', as in: *He provided details of the system whereby funds are transferred from one account to the other.*

It should not be used to mean 'in which', eg:

> ✗ *The situation has been created whereby people are actually afraid to join a trade union.*

which. See what.

wholly

Spelt with double *l*.

➤ See also **holey**.

who's or whose

The spellings are sometimes confused, so take care to use the correct form in writing.

- ○ **who's** is the short form of 'who is' or 'who has', as in: *Who's that at the door?* □ *Who's eaten all the chocolates?* Remember not to use this shortened form in formal writing.

- ○ **whose** is the possessive form of 'who', as in: *This is the boy whose mother was injured in the accident.* □ *Whose dirty socks are these? Whose* is also correctly used to mean 'of which', as in: *The tree, whose branches were home to many small creatures, blew down in the storm.*

wilful or willful

The first spelling is used in BrE, and the second only in AmE.

will. See shall.

wont. See want.

workable

Notice the ending is *-able* (not *-ible*).

works

The noun can take a singular or a plural verb, as in: *The works is/are closing down for a fortnight.*

wreath or wreathe

The form without the *e* is the noun, and the form with the *e* is the verb. Notice that when *-ing* and *-ed* are added to the verb this last *e* is dropped.

XYZ

-xion. See **-ction**.

X-ray

Spelt with capital *X* and a hyphen.

yoghourt, **yoghurt** and **yogurt**

All three spellings are correct, though *yoghurt* is the commonest.

your or **you're**

Take care to use the correct form in writing.

○ *your* is the possessive form of 'you', as in: *Are those your CDs?*

○ *you're* is the short form of 'you are', as in: *Come on, Isabel, you're next*. Try to avoid using this shortened form in formal business correspondence.

yours

Remember that there is no apostrophe in *yours*: *This book is yours, not mine*.

zabaglione

Pronounced /za-ba-**lyoh**-ni/. The *g* is silent.

zealot

Pronounced /**zel**-ot/.

zero

The plural is **zeros**.